Jazz Dance Training

WITHDRAWN

Dörte Wessel-Therhorn

Jazz Dance Training

Meyer & Meyer Sport

Original title: Jazz Dance Training
– Aachen: Meyer & Meyer Verlag, 1996
Translated by Peter Bereza and Heike Albert

British Library Cataloguing in Publication Data
A catalogue record for this book is available from the British Library

Wessel-Therhorn, Dörte:
Jazz dance training/Wessel-Therhorn [Transl.: Peter Bereza and Heike Albert].
2nd Ed.– Oxford : Meyer & Meyer Sport (UK) Ltd., 2000
ISBN 1-84126-041-X

© 1998 by Meyer & Meyer Sport (UK) Ltd.
2nd Edition 2000
Oxford, Aachen, Olten (CH), Vienna,
Québec, Lansing/Michigan, Adelaide, Auckland, Johannesburg, Budapest
Member of the World
Sportpublishers' Association
Photos: Wim Fischer, Mainz
Figures: Martin Görlich, Mainz
Cover design: Thomas Landini, Mainz / Birgit Engelen, Stolberg
Cover and type exposure: frw, Reiner Wahlen, Aachen
Editorial: Dr. Irmgard Jaeger, Aachen
Printed and bound in Germany by
Burg Verlag Gastinger GmbH, Stolberg
ISBN 1-84126-041-X
e-mail: verlag@meyer-meyer-sports.com

Table of Contents

Introduction

This book is based on an as yet unpublished manuscript describing the technique and method of *Jazz Dance* as developed by ALAIN BERNARD and documenting his life and achievements as a dancer, instructor and choreographer. It is to be translated and published as a *Jazz Dance* text book in Poland, where BERNARD started working in 1977 as the first *Jazz Dance* teacher and choreographer from the west.

ALAIN BERNARD, educated in Switzerland and in the USA, became the founder of *Jazz Dance* in Switzerland (from 1959) while he was still performing on stage himself. I first met him in 1971 in Bern, where he had organised an international summer course. Along with other courses, I had registered for *Jazz Dance* in order to study this style of performance dance for the first time. *Jazz Dance*, that "typically American child", characterized by tempo and dynamics and an expression which constantly changes and adapts itself to prevailing tastes as the years go by, is inherently fascinating and continues to have a strong attraction for Europeans, in spite of their completely different approach and attitude towards dance. And yet there is a close link between *Jazz Dance* and the dancer or dance teacher who expresses, designs or teaches it. And BERNARD has the ability, in his own special way, to convey both - the expression and the teaching of *Jazz Dance* - to the learner and to the dancer. He is the one who has influenced me most in my own work in this field of dance.

Jazz Dance is not so much a dance technique as a dance style which can assume a range of forms, depending on prevailing tastes. It contrasts strongly with classical ballet, with its essentially romantic character and aspiration to a technique which empowers it to overcome gravity, to break loose from earthbound human existence and to "rise above itself". *Jazz Dance* strives towards the ground, and no matter what classical or popular form it assumes, it comes first and foremost "from the guts" (cf. Giordano, 1992). From its original roots in Africa, it has evolved out of the rhythm and movement culture of black Americans. It continues to come from the people, from the street. It is emotional, sensual, lively, earthbound, funky, "crazy" and is constantly being reinvented. In the course of its evolution, it has developed into a style of performance dance which demands the utmost from the dancer, but at the same time it has also become widely popular among amateur dancers.

This is where the problem lies. *Jazz Dance* teachers, if they want to do a thoroughly good job, must base their *Jazz Dance* style on a dance technique which will enable dancers, whether in professional or amateur contexts, to start moving and expressing themselves appropriately.

It was BERNARD's special concern, from the very start of the development of European *Jazz Dance*, to school professional and especially amateur dancers in a basic physical and technical training routine which would enable them to use their body as an instrument in all its versatility and vitality. BERNARD developed his technique and his method on the basis of a modern dance training like that taught by MARTHA GRAHAM, whose student he was, and LESTER HORTON.

Modern Dance, whose most famous exponent is MARTHA GRAHAM, developed at the beginning of this century as a style of performance dance offering a radical alternative to classical ballet. In the course of its evolution, Modern Dance has also taken on a wide range of expressions and has been influenced by all dance styles, including classical ballet. Modern Dance training, as taught by GRAHAM and HORTON, involves extensive and systematically developed floor, barre, centre and locomotor exercises in order to cultivate the body into a complete "dance tool".

It is obvious that this kind of training on a modern basis is also highly suitable as a preparation for *Jazz Dance*. BERNARD accordingly devised a basic training concept fitting for *Jazz Dance* with which beginners can develop and gradually increase their stamina and technical coordination to meet the requirements.

The intention of this book is to document his work and to add my own experiences from my work in the field of *Jazz Dance*.

I hope that this book will represent a contribution to basic training in *Jazz Dance*. I am, however, fully aware that it can never be a substitute for the presence, personality and creativity of a teacher.

1 THE DEVELOPMENT OF JAZZ DANCE

The following chapter provides a short summary of the development of *Jazz Dance* from its folkloristic origins to an American performance dance style. Its aim is to enhance understanding in the teacher and in the dancer for the characteristics of this style of dance. The summary is based primarily on the book "Jazz Dance" by HELMUT GÜNTHER and on a manuscript about the "History of Jazz Dance" by ALAIN BERNARD which provide a comprehensive description of the development of Afro-American dance styles and their evolution into *Jazz Dance*, and which present famous representatives of *Jazz Dance* and their works.

1.1 Roots and Basic Characteristics

Jazz Dance, as it is also known today in Europe, consists of a vast variety of elements. It is a combination of the most varied dance styles and uses dance forms of different nations. Although this synthesis of ballet, modern dance, social and street dance, folklore and acrobatic dance puts almost no limits at all on the creativity of the choreographer, it has two absolutely essential elements: *polycentricism* and *polyrhythm*. Both originate in Africa and thus one can rightly claim that Africa is the true birthplace of *Jazz Dance*.

African culture is a dance, music and rhythm culture with its own aesthetic standards and a high state of development. Africans do not perform their dances out of any spontaneous improvisation. Dances follow strict choreographic forms which are thoroughly studied, passed on to the next generation and always danced in the same way. The African principles of movement and rhythm have now been well researched and form the essential basis of both Afro-American and Euro-American *Jazz Dance*.

The basic locomotor principle of *polycentricism*, which helps Africans to reach ecstatic states, is the absolute opposite of European dance forms, as is most obvious in the case of ballet. White dancers move their bodies primarily as a unit, with central control of the body in upright and tensed posture. The foremost aims are to overcome gravity and to achieve harmony and lightness.

Polycentricism, on the other hand, means that the body is isolated in separate parts, creating several centres of movement which each have their own individual and independent rhythm and space. This requires a certain degree of relaxation and tension in the isolated parts of the body and a special technique. A further important characteristic is the somewhat bent posture which underlines gravity and which is expressed in dance forms executed on the knees, in crouching or in lying. *Polycentricism* is the basic principle of African and Afro-American dance. While Africans have the isolation technique which helps to achieve *polycentricism*, and also *polyrhythmic* expression (i.e. several parts of the body are moved simultaneously but with different rhythms) in their blood, white dancers must first learn the techniques.

1.2 Origin and Development in America

The Afro-American history of dance and thus the early history of *Jazz Dance* has its beginnings in the arrival of the first African slaves in America, who brought their dances and rhythms along with them. They were permitted to show them at the rare feasts which their white masters allowed them to have. The polycentric dance forms of the large community of Bantu slaves from the Congo and Angola are regarded as the roots of *Jazz Dance* as it later became, while the rhythmic beating, sliding and stamping leg and foot techniques of the Africans from West African and the Sudan are associated more with the evolution of Tap Dance.

From 1820 on, white artists started to adopt the black dancing techniques, the African rhythms and the style, and to perform them as "minstrels" (white dancers, singers and musicians dressed and made-up as blacks). Gradually, black artists also joined in, and a mixture of white and black music and dancing styles ensued in which the assimilation of one cultural heritage into the other took place. The minstrels, who performed up to about 1900, made a contribution to the legitimacy of an Afro-American culture and laid the foundations of that typical American cultural uniqueness in the fields of music and dance so well-known today.

The terms *Jazz Music* and *Jazz Dance* appeared for the first time officially around 1915, first in Chicago and then also in New York. The word "jazz", however, was used by black Americans earlier than that, as a noun and as a verb. As a noun it originally meant power, ferociousness, ecstatic excitement. It is still used today as a verb in a large variety of meanings, e.g. *to jazz around, to jazz up*.

Jazz Music and *Jazz Dance* have a common history of origin. Dances with pelvic movements, twists and slides which were danced to jazz music were given the same name as the music. After the first successes of negro musicals on Broadway which popularized many new jazz dances later danced in ballrooms, black culture withdrew to Harlem in about 1900 in order to make musicals by blacks for blacks.

The second phase of negro musicals lasted from about 1921 to about 1930. It was the heyday of jazz music in Harlem. At the centre of the scene were the "Savoy" and the "Cotton Club", which produced famous musicians like Duke Ellington.

In the following period from 1931-1939, the time of America's economic crisis, the American dance and music scene was dominated by white artists. Well-known names from this era are, for example, Benny Goodman and his Big Band and the tap dancer Fred Astaire. A few black people began to show interest in classical ballet and Modern Dance and tried to turn the black style of dancing into a serious form of performance dance.

The first major break-through of black dancing as acknowledged performance dance came with the black dancer and choreographer KATHRIN DUNHAM, who was also a historian and ethnologist. She studied the dances of Haiti and the West Indies and thus became a champion of Afro-American dance culture. A new school of performance dance was born, dedicated to Afro-American culture. More and more black dancers joined in, choreographing and performing with their own groups in *Jazz Dance* style. The "Dunham School of Dance", founded in 1945, produced many renowned choreographers still remembered today. During the 40s, parallel to this development, white dancers trained in ballet and modern dance started taking over elements of black *Jazz Dance*. And so, gradually, the synthesis which we know today as American *Jazz Dance* came into being.

The foremost representatives of black *Jazz Dance* were GEOFFRY HOLDER, TALLEY BEATTY and ALVIN AILEY. Representatives of white *Jazz Dance* who had a great influence on the European development of *Jazz Dance* were JACK COLE, FRANK WAGNER and LUIGI and GUS GIORDANO. Choreographies like "West Side Story" by JEROME ROBBINS contributed to the fame and popularity all over Europe of *Jazz Dance* in the typical mixture of ballet, Modern Dance and acrobatic dance we know today. Worldwide acknowledgement of soul music and soul dance in the 1960s also helped to pave the way for *Jazz Dance* to spread to Europe.

1.3 The Spread of Jazz Dance in Europe

At the summer school in Krefeld in 1959, *Jazz Dance* was taught for the first time in Europe by the black dancer and dance teacher WALTER NICKS. His assistant was ALAIN BERNARD, who was later to become the father of *Jazz Dance* in Switzerland. Over the years, more and more teachers, black and also white, came from America to international dance academies in Europe, and a new synthesis came into being which evolved into European *Jazz Dance*.

Today, *Jazz Dance* is an integral part of every dancer's education. It has also become enormously popular with amateur dancers. In schools for amateur dancers, it is currently probably the most frequently taught dance style.

Jazz Dance is primarily a dance style which, like modern jazz, rock and pop music, is continuously undergoing changes. Thus, talented teachers and choreographers will inevitably, on the basis of their education as dancers, create their own individual styles. The extent to which they will be able to realize such dance styles with amateur dancers will, however, depend on basic training. A good modern basic training is needed to help amateur dancers to develop their dance technique and their stamina, so that they can rise to the challenges of the choreography.

2 THE TEACHING CONCEPT

2.1 Who this Book Is for and What It Aims to Do

The following descriptions of functional basics, exercise forms, model lessons and series of exercises in *Jazz Dance* are intended for everyone who is interested in *Jazz Dance*, but especially for teachers, instructors and dance trainers who are looking for a sound basis on which to plan their training and material for a basic course in dancing. This could be for a beginner class in *Jazz Dance*, perhaps at a sports club, at university, in a school workshop, or in a dance studio. It could also be for groups who already have dancing experience in other areas.

The basis of any dance activity which aims to be more than a private, unstructured movement or a random-spontaneous self-presentation is a full awareness of the body as a "dance instrument". In order to apply a dance style optimally, dancers, whether professional or amateur, must prepare their bodies consciously and comprehensively so that they can be used like an instrument with virtuosity and expressiveness.

Suppleness, elasticity, a high degree of mobility and strength in its various manifestations as well as basic dance techniques must be developed systematically over a longer period of time. And it is essential that the work is functionally correct and economical. Only in this way can overloads be avoided which may lead to damage and injuries, and dancers be enabled to achieve optimal mobility and expression. Dancers must be able, at any moment during the dance, to centre their bodies, to correctly position and monitor all parts of the body and to apply energy in whatever form and quantity that moment requires.

This all needs an adequate phase of focusing and warming-up, an intensive programme of stretching and strengthening, and good technical coordination training involving the whole body, the entire organism with all its possibilities and functions.

It is the teacher's task to tune the dance training to these requirements. The teacher must

- *teach the students to use their bodies consciously,*
- *equip them through special exercises and correction with the techniques to execute movements correctly and optimally,*
- *help them to increase their dancing skills and repertoire by gradually increasing the challenge, for example through faster performance of the exercises, increasing numbers of exercises, variations of exercises, greater complexity, new combinations as well as more frequent and longer training units.*

2.2 The Materials

The following range of functional basics, collections of exercises, exercise selections and hints on how to structure them can be used to design a basic training programme which will achieve the aims mentioned above.

Anatomical-functional Basics

This chapter teaches the most important facts relating to the building up of posture and to the mobility of the body as a unit and in its parts. It also deals with the most important criteria for training mobility, strength and balance. It describes the isolation technique as the basis for polycentric movements. In this way the foundations are laid for an understanding of the issues and for the application of the catalogue of exercises.

The Catalogue of Exercises

The catalogue of exercises represents the repertoire of exercises in ALAIN BERNARD's classes and ranges from simple basic exercises and techniques for beginners to complicated combinations for advanced students. These series of exercises are not arranged according to level of difficulty but to the working position in space (centre, floor, barre, etc.), which also reflect the methodological sequence within one lesson. Each exercise is first described in terms of its effect and its precise technical execution. To provide a quick survey of the level of difficulty of individual exercise options for the lessons, a grading is given which also relates to the model lessons.

The Model Lessons

The two model lessons show how a beginners' course is structured according to BERNARD's approach, and which exercises or parts of exercises from the catalogue of exercises can be used. The first example describes one of the first lessons in a group totally unfamiliar with *Jazz Dance*. The second example provides guidance on the development of exercise forms, how often they should be performed and in what sequence after about 6-8 months of training.

Drawing on her experience with beginner classes, the author has added notes on typical sources of errors, advice on how to correct and examples of music.

2.3 The Lessons

2.3.1 The Structure of a Lesson

If possible one training unit, i.e. one dance lesson, should run for 90 minutes if it is to be effective. This is assumed in the following model course plan for levels 1-3, as given in BERNARD's catalogue of exercises:

1. Centre Work 1
This part of the lesson serves to warm-up the learners, focus them and build up their posture through movements of the whole body while standing.

2. Floor Work 1
In the first phase of floor work, the emphasis is on exercises which raise awareness of the unity of breathing and movement, which train general flexibility and which prepare both the flex-stretch coordination of the legs and the *contractions*.

3. Barre
The next work phase at the barre consists of passive, active, static and dynamic stretching exercises, and prepares for techniques like *turns, lay outs and falls* with balance support.

4. Floor Work 2
In the second phase of floor work, the focus is primarily on developing the strength of the torso and the leg muscles, and preparing dance postures and gestures of the leg, such as *passé, attitude, developpé, battement, and rond de jambe*.

5. Centre Work 2 and Isolation
The second phase of open space work consists of exercises to develop and perfect balance and torsion and to practise the technique of isolation as a stylistic trait of *Jazz Dance*.

6. Across the Floor
The next phase is work across the floor, either diagonally as the longest distance in the room, or across the middle, to practise the combinations of steps, jumps and turns in rhythmical entries and sequences.

Rounding off

A dance lesson is always rounded off with an exercise for active relaxation, for example loose swinging out, rolling the body down and up, or breathing consciously while pulling the body together and straightening up.

2.3.2 Teaching and Learning Methods

The form of basic dance training according to BERNARD presented in this book espouses an exclusively deductive approach in a frontal lesson. When doing floor work or centre work, participants stand, lie or sit well distributed around the room, leaving enough space between each other and facing the teacher and/or the mirror. At the barre, they face the barre or stand with their sides to it. If the group is too big and there is not enough room, two groups can be formed which work alternately. The "passive" group, however, must remain involved in the lesson and stay warm. Fast changes between the groups are appropriate here. When doing locomotor exercises (across the floor), participants usually line up in rows of 2 or 4 along one wall or in one corner of the room so that they can each have a specified time to practise the combinations of steps, jumps or turns alone.

The teacher uses demonstration, explanation, shouts and rhythmical instructions to teach the students how to move. Repetitive practice helps them to gradually perfect the movements. Correction by the teacher is oral and tactile, and there is also the feedback given by the mirror. This approach, in which instructions and demonstrations prevail, requires teachers or instructors to be able, at least on an elementary level, to demonstrate the exercises precisely, and to have exact knowledge of the technical characteristics and functional conditions of the exercises. They must also be able to master the rhythmical sequences and divide them into short, supportive instructions. They must provide general and individual correction and must know the potentials and the limits of the particular learning groups.

2.3.3 Levels and Focuses of Practice

Normally *Jazz Dance* classes are divided into three major levels: Beginners, Intermediate and Advanced. To do more justice to the range of starting levels and to the progress of the learners, the levels can be subdivided into Beginners I+II,

Intermediate I+II and Advanced I+II. This system is based on the American approach, which regards *Jazz Dance* primarily as a dance style, and which assumes some basic dancing skills from the very start. When assigning learners to course levels, it is essential to differentiate between absolute newcomers to dance and newcomers to *Jazz Dance*. In the catalogue of exercises, in the model lessons and in the practice series of this book which deals mostly with basic training at beginner level, gradings are also given and defined in detail each time.

At beginner levels, most of the time is taken up with training posture basics and building up the learners' stamina and technical coordination, the basic requirements for dancing. The learning of steps and dance combinations takes second place. As the learners advance and develop more physical and technical potential, the focus changes and increasingly more time is devoted to jazz stylistic exercises *(afro-primitive, latin-jazz, musical, modern, hip hop, etc.)*, to bigger and faster combinations *(jazz combinations)*, to leaps, turns and fast changes across several spatial planes *(falls)* and to more challenging balance forms. Finally these exercises can evolve into choreographies, which can be performed by a group. The quality of the work at advanced level depends on the solid basic training of the learners and the pedagogic and artistic skills of the teacher.

3 BASIC TRAINING

3.1. Anatomical-functional Basics for Dance Training

3.1.1. Posture Awareness and Straightening

The starting point of all work to develop dance qualities is the training of learners' awareness of and ability to maintain posture in terms of correct straightening. Straightening up is a form of movement against the force of gravity. An upright posture is achieved through straightening and holding muscles and through a constant struggle between one's own muscular strength and the earth's gravitational pull.

A fully upright posture while standing looks like this:
   The spine with its double S-form is stretched as far as possible vertically and flattened, the pelvis is straight, shoulder girdle, pelvic girdle, knee and foot joints make one vertical line, the sternum is slightly lifted and the neck is stretched upwards. The perpendicular runs from the vertex down through the vertebrae of the neck and the region of the lumbar vertebrae, and ends at a point between the feet at the height of the axis of the ankle joints. All straightening muscles, mainly the back extensor and the stomach muscles, the gluteus maximus and the anterior and posterior muscles of the legs are equally tensed.

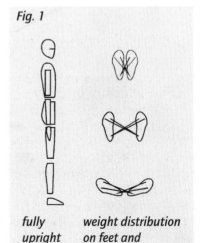

Fig. 1

   The foundation of this posture are the feet in parallel position. The weight is equally distributed on three points: the ball of the big toe, the ball of the small toe and the heel. The plantar arch is upright, and the instep does not touch the floor. The drawings on the right illustrate a fully upright posture and how weight is distributed on the feet.

fully upright posture   *weight distribution on feet and perpendicular*

This posture is the dancer's starting position in all exercises relating to statics and kinetics. It allows a functional execution of the exercises and expresses the body's readiness to transfer weight easily and swiftly, to move in all directions, to use its parts in isolation and to maintain balance.

3.1.2 Stability and Strength of the Torso

To be able to stabilize and apply the torso optimally in turns, leaps, balance moments, contractions and fast changes across different spatial planes, the muscles of the torso must be well trained, especially the back muscles, the buttocks and the stomach.

The large muscles of the torso, which primarily serve static purposes, are subject to different conditions than those of the muscles of the extremities. Exercises aimed at strengthening these muscle groups must be designed accordingly.

Training must take into consideration the different ways in which muscle strengthening works and must provide, on the one hand, exercises involving isometrics, i.e. maintaining a position without visible change of muscle length, and also dynamic exercises which shorten or lengthen the muscles through concentric and excentric practice. With respect to the muscles of the torso, it makes sense to perform exercises calmly and over a longer period of time with breaks. When choosing exercises to strengthen the stomach muscles, make sure that the lumbar vertebrae are not put under incorrect or excessive strain.

3.1.3 Flexibility of the Torso

The locomotor system of the torso consists of the spine, the pelvis and the shoulder girdle as a functional unit.

Movements within the torso are realized primarily in the spine and supported by movements of the shoulder girdle.

The spine, the vertical axis in the body, is a column divided into different sections and is both solid and elastic at the same time. It consists of a large number of individual parts and has a characteristic double S-curve in the front-back plane (sagittal plane). These curves are physiological and necessary to absorb and dampen shocks, such as those delivered when a dancer executes a leap. Five sections are distinguished according to the regions of the body: cervical vertebrae, dorsal vertebrae, lumbar vertebrae, sacrum and coccyx. Various movements can take place in isolation in these different sections (see "Technique of Isolation"), but the spine can also move as a unit with all its parts moving interdependently. The main reference planes of movement are derived from the spatial dimensions.

Planes of Movement

- *Sagittal plane:*   This runs vertically from front to back in the upright body. The movements of flexing and stretching take place in this plane.
- *Frontal plane:*   This runs vertically from side to side in the upright body. Abduction and adduction take place in this plane.
- *Transversal plane:* This runs horizontally in the upright body. Inward rotation and outward rotation take place in this plane.

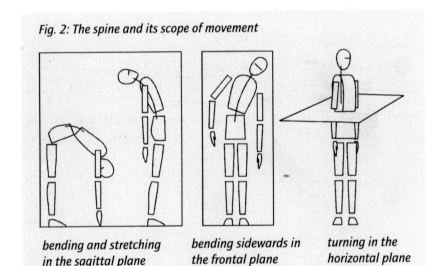

Fig. 2: The spine and its scope of movement

bending and stretching in the sagittal plane   *bending sidewards in the frontal plane*   *turning in the horizontal plane*

Main Locomotor Directions of the Spine

- Bending and stretching in the sagittal plane (front-back direction)
- Bending sidewards in the frontal plane (side-side direction)
- Turning or rotating around the vertical axis in the transversal plane.

When dancing, all planes of movement and movement potentials of the spine are used and thus need to be extensively trained. Stretching exercises in the main planes of movement can be supported by strengthening the pulling power of the arms. It is essential to make sure in exercises that the individual planes are correctly maintained and that movements are controlled. A high level of strain through wide amplitudes of movement which go close to the limit, movements in combined planes and fast execution of movements should only be attempted after a thorough warm-up in advanced classes. Basically, any jerky, sharp movements, frequent and excessive stretching of the lumbar vertebrae and excessively large, fast circular movements of the head should be avoided.

3.1.4 Mobility, Stretching and Coordination of the Lower Extremities

An optimal if not maximal locomotor width of both bent and stretched legs in the hip joints is necessary for expressive poses, gestures and movements in dance.

Basic Leg Movements in the Hip Joint

- Bending and stretching in the sagittal plane (front-back direction)
- Spreading out and bringing back in the frontal plane (side-side direction)
- Inward and outward rotation in the transversal plane
- Rotation of the leg (circumduction) through several planes, for specific dance movements also combined with inward and outward rotation.

Fig. 3: Basic leg movements in the hip joint

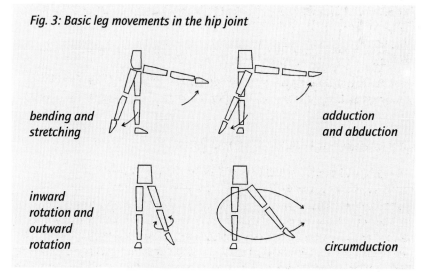

bending and stretching

adduction and abduction

inward rotation and outward rotation

circumduction

The extent of the movement of the leg in the hip joint alone is difficult to ascertain, since almost all movements of the lower extremities can be complemented, and sometimes even replaced, by the pelvis and the vertebrae connected with it. Thus large, wide leg movements are always accompanied by additional movements and balancing movements with the pelvis and the lumbar vertebrae. Such movements should, however, be avoided as much as possible during training. The teacher must therefore ensure through correction that pelvis and spine are fixed along their axis and that movements are executed with precision.

Types of Mobility

- *Passive mobility:*   Amplitude of movement is achieved through the effect of external force.
- *Active mobility:*   Amplitude of movement is achieved through the dancer's own muscular strength.

A high degree of mobility can be achieved through specific stretching of muscles and tendons. Since the diverse requirements of dance must be fulfilled, all methods of stretching must be considered. It is important to note that the special standards required for dancing are not identical with the standards of general functional gymnastics.

Types of Stretching Exercises

- Passive stretching exercises: through the effect of external force (body weight, partner, devices)
- Active stretching exercises: through muscle work of the antagonist
- Static stretching exercises: maintenance of a specific amplitude of movement
- Dynamic stretching exercises: rhythmic alternation between greater and lesser amplitude
- Combination of all forms

To develop the muscles thoroughly and to enable them to meet the wide variety of demands in dance, all kinds of stretching should be applied and combined with each other, for example *passive-static* exercises (held, deep front lunge or split), or *active-dynamic* exercises (high thrusts of the leg). What counts most in dancing is active mobility on the basis of a good passive amplitude of movement. To achieve and maintain the stretching of a muscle, daily training and several repetitions are necessary. Before doing active-dynamic exercises with stretched legs at the limits of movement amplitude, learners must first do a thorough warm-up. Learners should never perform the exercises jerkily and should not go over the pain threshold, since micro-tears, pulled muscles and other injuries may be the consequence.

Position and Interplay of the Joints

The interplay of the leg and foot joints along one single common axis is essential for the functional execution of a movement so that excessive strain or injury is avoided and the whole locomotor apparatus can be fully applied. False axial strain on the leg and foot joints also result in incorrect posture and strain on the spine.

When the strain on the supporting leg is correctly distributed, the knee joint is vertically above the foot joint, the foot rests on three points, and the plantar arch is upright (see section on "Posture Work" chap. 3.1.1). When the leg is bent, the knee shifts forward exactly over the toes; in toe stand the weight is shifted more onto the big toe and the second toe to prevent the foot joint from bending outwards.

The inward and outward rotation of the leg is started from the hip joint. The position of the lower leg and the foot results from this and depends on an ability to roll the hip joint out or in. All movements with the free leg are also subject to these functional laws.

Dance movements also require well-developed *bend-stretch coordination* of the legs, for example in leaps in which the supporting leg bends in the landing phase, while the free leg is held backwards in a stretched and upright position (*arabesque*). To achieve this coordination precisely according to the functional aspects described above, special and conscious practice is required.

3.1.5 Balance and Turns

An essential aspect of training the whole range of dance forms is the perfecting of the ability to stay in equilibrium, to *maintain and recover balance under changing circumstances*. This might be through forms of movement with a very small supporting surface (for example on the balls of the feet, on the hip, on the hand) or with unstable balance conditions (shifting the torso out of the axis, fast or large changes of position from one spatial plane to the other, turns, etc.). Improvement of balance depends to a great extent on an effective training of support motorics and on sensitization and refinement of analytic perceptors (optical, kinesthetical, tactile, etc.). It is therefore important to achieve a state of *being accustomed to exceptional situations* through active practice, repetition, variation, combination and through expansion of the range of movements. In this way, reactions to these unusual situations become faster, more controlled and economic, more precisely oriented and more varied.

For balance, it is essential to practise stabilization of the torso including the pelvis, and precise distribution of weight on the areas of support (see section on "Torso Stability" chap. 3.1.2). At beginner levels this skill can best be trained with the help of the barre.

   To be able to turn around the vertical axis in a variety of ways (for example double footed, single footed, in the air, with varying positions of the free leg) while maintaining orientation, a special technique must be learnt during basic training. The technique of turning consists basically of the phases *preparation*, the *rotatory start*, the *turn* itself and the *finish*.

The *preparation* (*préparation*) may consist of various foot positions or may develop from steps. It creates favourable starting positions through a slight lowering of the centre of gravity (*demi plié*) and a special position of the arms. The arm of the turning side is usually stretched out to the front and the other arm opened sideways.

In the explosive *rotatory start*, where strength must be appropriate to the degree and the speed of the turn, the weight is brought vertically over the supporting leg (or both legs) and lifted, the eyes fixed on one spot in the room. In the *turn* which follows directly, the arms are quickly closed from their open position and the whole body tenses to fix the complete posture. To maintain visual orientation, head and eyes are used as controlling mechanisms: the eyes are fixed for as long as possible on the same spot, while the torso turns frontwards. The increasing tension of the neck muscles is released suddenly and the head turns swiftly, overtaking the torso. As soon as possible, the eyes are fixed again on the same spot or a new spot in the room. At the end of the turn, the arms are opened again or brought into a new position. This slows the movement down and balances out the new situation. Then the weight is usually brought down in a *demi plié*.

   The technical elements described above should first be practised separately with balance support and partial turns (1/4 and 1/2 turns).

3.2 Isolation Technique

One aspect of the polycentric style of movement in *Jazz Dance* is the ability to use parts of the body in isolation. This body technique is natural to the African way of moving and must be learnt by white dancers. In the isolation technique, the body is divided into isolation centres whose basic movements are first trained separately. As the level of proficiency progresses, two or more of these centres are combined with each other at different speeds and rhythms (*polycentricity, polyrhythm*). The movements should be practised as flowing (*legato*) movements and as rapped (*staccato*) movements.

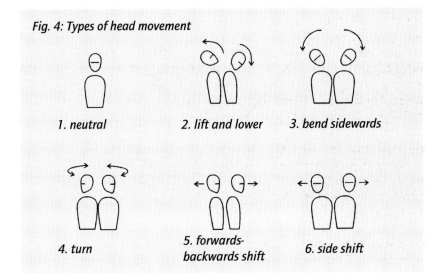

Fig. 4: Types of head movement

1. neutral   2. lift and lower   3. bend sidewards

4. turn   5. forwards-backwards shift   6. side shift

3.2.1 The Head as the Centre of Movement

Head movements are related to the flexibility of the cervical vertebrae and head joints which involves all planes. We therefore differentiate between the following types of head movements:

- Lifting and lowering or bending and stretching in the sagittal plane
- Bending sidewards in the frontal plane
- Turning diagonally and in profile in the transversal plane
- Shifting front-back-side-diagonal in the horizontal plane.

The combination of several of these types of movement may produce half circles and full circles. These should, however, be kept small and executed slowly and with good control, since uncontrolled and fast movements may result in damage of the small joints at each side of the cervical vertebrae or in a loss of balance.

3.2.2 The Shoulder Girdle as the Centre of Movement

The shoulder girdle is an open ring consisting of shoulder blades and collar bones, which is only connected with the sternum through muscles at the back and a joint at the front. This form gives it the high degree of flexibility required for the tasks of the upper extremities.

Types of Shoulder Girdle Movement

- Lift and lower
- Release – contract
- Half circle back and front
- Full circle back and front

Each shoulder can be moved separately in these ways; both shoulders can be moved parallel and in opposite directions. A typical jazz movement is the *shoulder shake*, a fast front-back shake which is transferred to the torso.

3.2.3 The Chest as the Centre of Movement

This centre is the most difficult one to move in isolation, since it is a part of the torso which is not very flexible at all. It is therefore difficult to exclude accompanying movement of the shoulder girdle and the pelvic girdle. For this reason it is necessary in training to fix the shoulder and pelvic girdles. It is also important in the neutral position to lift the chest as far as possible.

Types of Chest Movement

- Release – contract
- Side shift right and left
- Diagonal shift
- Circle

3.2.4 The Pelvis as the Centre of Movement

Isolated movements of the pelvis and the hips are particularly characteristic of the African origins of *Jazz Dance*. The pelvis can be easily moved in all directions through the combined mobility of the lumbar vertebrae and the hip joints. The movements of the pelvis can be isolated by bending the leg and hip joints and maximally *relaxing* the muscles and ligaments which normally serve a static function for the pelvic girdle.

Types of Pelvic Movement

- Release – contract
- Side shift
- Diagonal shift
- Circle right and left

These basic movements can be varied in many ways, with the emphasis on one side, in half-circles, in a cross, a square or a diamond.

3.2.5 The Arms

The arm consists of upper arm, lower arm and hand. The arm as a whole is moved at the shoulder joint, a ball joint with freedom of movement in all directions. Further movements take place at the elbow joint, the hand joint and the finger joints. The interplay of all these joints enable the arm and the hand to produce a wide variety of positions, movements and gestures.

But first some general remarks about arm movements in *Modern Dance* training. *The port de bras*, i.e. the movements of the arms in *Modern Dance* as understood by ALAIN BERNARD and others, are not peripheral gestures. They develop in the torso. Thus "open the arms side", for example, is an expansion from the centre of the torso, the "arm lift" results from pulling down the shoulderblades. Only in *"arm isolations"* are the arm movements of purely peripheral character.

The various basic positions used in *Jazz Dance* are shown under the rubric "standard terms and body positions", in Fig. 12.

3.2.6 The Legs

The leg consists of thigh, lower leg and foot. It is moved as a whole at the hip joint, whose scope of movement is described in section 3.1.4. The knee joint can be bent and stretched. When it is bent it can also be rotated. The upper ankle joint permits bending and stretching movements. In addition, the foot is capable of circumduction through the combination of several joints. Bending the foot or "pulling it up" (dorsal flexion) is called *"flex"* in *Jazz Dance* exercises; stretching the foot downwards (plantar flexion) is called *"point"*. It is also very important in the dance to consciously use the phalanges in these movements. When all the leg joints are combined, the free leg can produce a variety of leg poses and leg gestures. Whether *Jazz Dance* works with parallel, inwards or outwards rolled leg positions in the free leg as well as in the supporting leg, attention must be given to the maintenance of the perpendicular position of the joints (see section 3.1.4). The basic positions of the feet and the leg are shown under the rubric "standard terms and body positions", in Fig. 7-9 and Fig. 11.

3.3 Standard Terms and Body Positions

3.3.1 Lying Level   Fig. 5.1-4

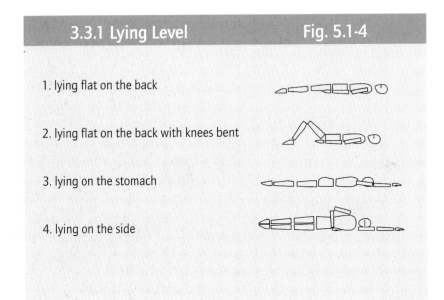

1. lying flat on the back

2. lying flat on the back with knees bent

3. lying on the stomach

4. lying on the side

3.3.2 Sitting Level   Fig. 6.1-8

1. sitting with legs closed (position 1)
2. sitting with legs open (position 2)
3. sitting with feet touching each other
   (V-position)
4. sitting with crossed legs
5. *swastika* (position 4)
6. *crossed swastika* (position 5)
7. *coccyx balance*
8. *jazz split*

3.3.3 Standing Level   Fig. 7

1. 1st position parallel
2. 2nd position parallel
3. 1st position with knees
   turned out, *demi plié*
4. 1st position with knees
   bent and turned out, *grand plié*
5. 2nd position with knees
   turned out, arms in V-position
6. 2nd position with knees
   bent and turned out, *demi plié*

Fig. 8

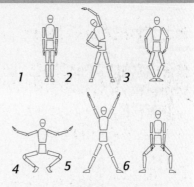

7. *flat back, table top position*
8. *flat back, table top position, demi plié*
9. *flat back*, diagonal front
10. *flat back, back bend*
11. *passé* parallel
12. *tendu* turned out side

Fig. 9

13. Foot *cou-de-pied*, front
14. *relevé* and *passé*, turned out
15. *attitude* side
16. *arabesque*
17. *lunge position* front
18. deep *lunge position*
19. *lunge position* side

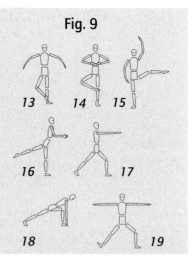

3.3.4 Kneeing Level   Fig. 10.1-7

1. knee sit
2. knee sit with *contraction*
3. knee sit with *release*
4. knee stand
5. knee stand, *hinch position*
6. knee stand with *table top position*
7. knee stand with *high release*

3.3.5 Foot Positions   Fig. 11

1. 1st position parallel
2. 2nd position parallel
3. 4th position parallel
4. 5th (3rd) position parallel
5. 1st position turned out
6. 2nd position turned out
7. 4th position turned out
8. 5th (3rd) position turned out

3.3.6 Arm Positions   Fig. 12.1-11

1. basic position, *long jazz arms*
2. 2nd position, *long jazz arms*
3. V-position
4. 3rd position, *long jazz arms*
5. basic position, classical arms
6. 2nd position, classical arms
7. 3rd position, classical arms
8. 1st position, *jazz arms*
9. 2nd position, *jazz arms*
10. 3rd position, *jazz arms*
11. V-position, *long jazz arms*

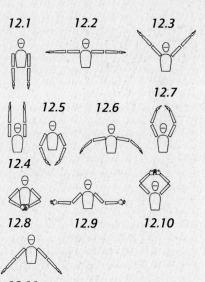

3.3.7 Spatial Directions

In Figure 13 the spatial directions in which dancers can turn or move are shown numbered clockwise starting from the position of the audience. Use of these numbers to denote direction makes it easier for the teacher to describe the movements and to give instructions.

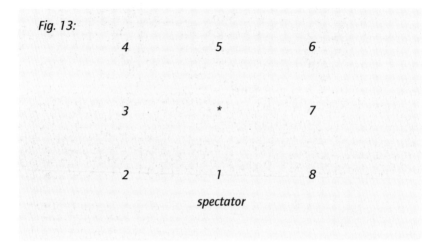

Fig. 13:

4	5	6
3	*	7
2	1	8

spectator

3.4 Catalogue of Exercises

Each exercise is first described in terms of its technical characteristics, its precise execution and its effect, and a grading is given in terms of level of difficulty. Grades 1+2 are for beginner levels. These may sometimes also be applicable at intermediate level (symbolized by↑) and they are also used in Model Lessons 1+2. Grade 3 denotes exercises for intermediate levels and above. The subsequent summary, number and chronological sequence of the individual exercises is very concise and assumes knowledge of all that has been so far stated. "Torso" means chest and pelvis unless otherwise defined. The numbers in brackets behind individual sequences of movement refer to the corresponding figures to the right of the exercise descriptions.

3.4.1 Centre Work 1

Exercise 1: "Roll Down And Up"

Abbreviations

counts	cts.
figure	Fig.
starting position	SP

Effect
Release and *contraction* of the torso muscles with bending and stretching of the spine. Development of posture in standing position.

Level of difficulty
Grade 1 ↑

Technical characteristics and execution
While standing straight upright, the vertebrae are rolled down one after the other, starting from the neck. The arms hang loosely under the shoulder girdle. The muscles of the back, the buttocks and the rear leg muscles are performing eccentric work here (see p. 23). Then the individual vertebrae are rolled up again, with pelvis, shoulder girdle and head being brought up one after the other into the perpendicular with a good deal of tension in the abdominals and buttocks and regular breathing out and in.
Starting position: stand, 2nd position parallel, Fig.14.1.

cts. Sequence	Fig. 14.1+14.2

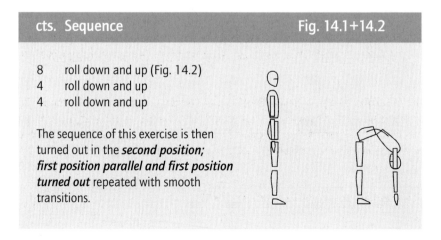

8   roll down and up (Fig. 14.2)
4   roll down and up
4   roll down and up

The sequence of this exercise is then turned out in the *second position; first position parallel and first position turned out* repeated with smooth transitions.

EXERCISE 2: "BEND AND BOUNCE AND PULLS"

Terms
flat backs	bending the torso backwards while the back is stretched
table top	torso parallel to the floor

Effect
This exercise in which three different torso positions are linked in direct interchange, serves primarily to stretch the spine and lengthen the muscles of the torso and of the rear leg. At the same time, the muscles of the torso are strengthened, especially the back extensors in the *flat back* position.

Level of difficulty
Grade 2 ↑ (for grade 1 in simplified version, see Model Lesson 1)

Technical characteristics and execution
1. Pull the rounded torso down towards the legs and bounce, reinforcing the movement with the arms. Make sure that the weight is not shifted onto the heels.

2. Bend the torso forwards with *flat back* and bounce, holding the arms in the second and third position. Make sure that the pelvis is not shifted back in order to balance out the weight of the torso, and that the legs are kept straight.

3. Straighten up the torso, turning the upper torso to the right and to the left with upwards pulls of the arm. Fix the pelvis in the neutral position, pull the shoulder blades down towards the spine. The feet develop counterpressure to the floor.

4. *Pulls:* With an upwards pull of one arm and downwards pull of the leg on the same side, the expansion of the torso and the stretching of the spine from the waist are intensified. The weight is shifted from one side to the other, with the foot rolling down from ball to heel and the knee bent.

Starting position: stand, 2nd position parallel.

cts. Sequence   Fig. 15.1+15.2

8	bounce deeply 8 times with rounded back (Fig. 15.1)
8	bounce deeply 8 times with *flat back*, arms in 2nd position (Fig. 15.2)
8	bounce 8 times to the right with straight torso (Fig. 15.3)

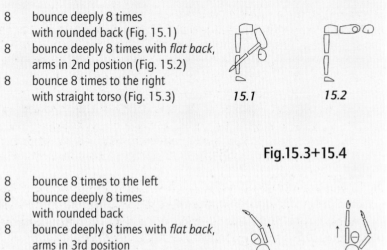

15.1   *15.2*

Fig.15.3+15.4

8	bounce 8 times to the left
8	bounce deeply 8 times with rounded back
8	bounce deeply 8 times with *flat back*, arms in 3rd position
8	8 *pulls* to the right and left alternately with straight torso (Fig. 15.4)

Repeat the whole sequence over
4 and 2 counts. The transitions from one
torso position to the next are continuous.

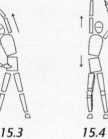

15.3   *15.4*

EXERCISE 3: "FLATBACKS"

Terms

flat backs	bending the torso backwards while the back is stretched
plié	bending the legs
relevé	lifting into ball and toe stand ("half points")

Effect

Flat backs are a technique developed by LESTER HORTON: They are executed frontwards, backwards and diagonally across, and develop static torso strength, bending and stretching mobility in the hip joints, and also sense of balance in *relevé positions*.

Level of difficulty
Grade 3 (for grades 1+2 in simplified version, see Model Lesson 1+2)

Technical characteristics and execution
1. *Flat backs* front: The torso is tensed and completely stretched, bent down to *table top* position or to diagonal position, and then straightened up again. The head stays in the same line as the spine, with the neck stretched. This exercise is executed with the arms in the second and third position. It can be made more difficult by means of *pliés* and *relevés*. In *pliés*, the back must be stretched and parallel to the floor and the plantar arch must be consciously pulled up. Straightening the back in *relevé* requires a high degree of tension in all muscles, which is further increased when the heels are pushed down and the body is consciously stretched upwards. This technique provides special training for balance.
2. In *flat backs* diagonally across front, the torso is dropped with a turn to one of the legs (the legs are in the 2nd position parallel or turned out). The weight remains on both feet throughout, the hip of the other side is consciously pulled back to produce an increased sidewards lengthening of the torso.
3. *Flat back back bends* are started by shifting the pelvis forward far over the feet, with the back kept stretched and the arms and head in line with the back. Straightening up is achieved by shifting back the centre of gravity and tensing the abdominals.
   All movements must be carried out slowly, controlled and with regular coordination of breathing.

Starting position: stand, 2nd position parallel, arms in basic position.

cts.	Sequence	Fig. 16.1-2
4	bend the stretched torso	
4	straighten up the stretched torso	
4	bend the stretched torso,	
	arms in 3rd position (Fig. 16.1)	*16.1*
4	straighten up the stretched torso	
4	bend the stretched torso, *plié* (Fig. 16.2)	
4	stretch legs	
4	straighten up the stretched torso	*16.2*

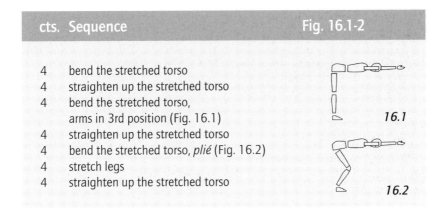

cts.	Sequence (continued)	Fig. 16.3+17.1-3

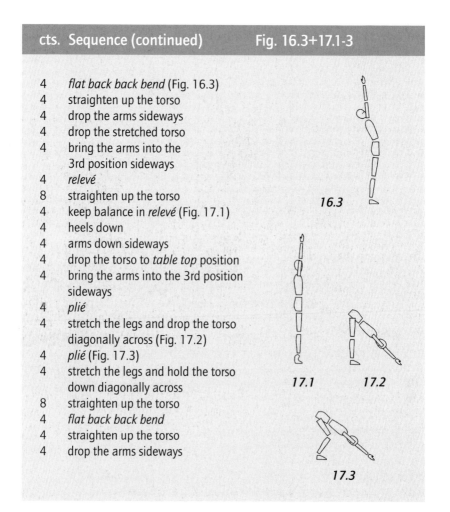

4	*flat back back bend* (Fig. 16.3)
4	straighten up the torso
4	drop the arms sideways
4	drop the stretched torso
4	bring the arms into the 3rd position sideways
4	*relevé*
8	straighten up the torso
4	keep balance in *relevé* (Fig. 17.1)
4	heels down
4	arms down sideways
4	drop the torso to *table top* position
4	bring the arms into the 3rd position sideways
4	*plié*
4	stretch the legs and drop the torso diagonally across (Fig. 17.2)
4	*plié* (Fig. 17.3)
4	stretch the legs and hold the torso down diagonally across
8	straighten up the torso
4	*flat back back bend*
4	straighten up the torso
4	drop the arms sideways

16.3

17.1   *17.2*

17.3

3.4.2 Floor Work 1

EXERCISE 4: "BOUNCES AND ISOLATIONS"

Terms

flex-point	bending (dorsal flexion) and stretching (plantar flexion) the foot

Effect
The following exercises improve the flexibility of the spine and bending and abduction in the hip joint. The muscles of the back of the leg and the adductors are lengthened passively-dynamically (see p. 23) to improve bending and spreading abilities.

Level of difficulty
Grade 3 (for grade 1+2 in simplified version, see Model Lesson 1+2)

Technical characteristics and execution
In different sitting positions the torso, starting at its centre rounded and stretched, is bounced forwards and to the sides. Then the upright chest is moved right and left, forwards and backwards in isolation. The pelvis stays in the neutral position throughout. In the second sitting position the legs stay rolled out and fully stretched, the feet are *flexed* with the heels not touching the floor. The arms are held in various positions or used to lengthen the torso sideways by means of pulls.

Starting position: sitting upright, soles of the feet touching each other.

cts. Sequence   Fig. 18.1-5+19.1

8	bounce rounded torso forwards 8 times (Fig.18.1)
8	bounce stretched torso forwards 8 times, arms in 1st position (Fig 18.2)

18.1

8	bounce forward 8 times alternating between rounded and stretched torso
8	shift chest 8 times to the right and to the left in upright position (isolation), arms in 2nd position

SP: stretch and close legs for 1st sitting position, point feet

18.2

8	bounce rounded torso forwards 8 times (Fig 18.3)

18.3

8	bounce stretched torso forwards 8 times, arms in 1st position, feet are flexed (Fig. 18.4)
8	bounce 8 times alternating between rounded and stretched torso, *point* feet when torso is round, *flex* feet when torso is stretched

18.4

8	shift chest 8 times to the right and to the left (isolation), arms in 2nd position

SP: open stretched legs for 2nd sitting position, point feet

8	bounce rounded torso forwards 8 times (Fig. 18.5)

18.5

8	bounce stretched torso forwards 8 times, *flex* feet, arms in V-position (Fig. 19.1)
8	bounce 8 times alternating between rounded and stretched torso, and between *pointed* and *flexed* feet (see above)

19.1

cts. Sequence (continued)   Fig. 19.2-5

8   shift chest to the right and
     to the left 8 times (isolation),
     arms in 2nd position

8   bounce rounded torso 8 times
     over right leg, *point* feet (Fig.19.2)

19.2

8   bounce stretched torso 8 times
     over right leg, *flex* feet, arms in
     1st position (Fig. 19.3)

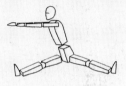

8   bounce 8 times alternating
     between rounded and stretched torso,
     and between *pointed* and *flexed* feet

8   bounce rounded torso 8 times
     over left leg, *point* feet

19.3

8   bounce stretched torso 8 times
     over left leg, arms in 1st position

8   bounce 8 times alternating between
     rounded and stretched torso, and
     between *pointed* and *flexed* feet

8   shift chest forwards and backwards
     8 times (isolation), hands to the groin

8   bounce upright torso 8 times to the right,
     left arm in 3rd position (Fig. 19.4)

19.4

4   circle torso forwards then
     to the left side

8   bounce torso to the left 8 times,
     right arm in 3rd position (Fig.19.5)

2   straighten up torso, arms in
     2nd position

8   bounce torso to the right 8 times, *flex* feet,
     left arm in 3rd position

19.5

2   straighten up torso, arms in
     2nd position

8   bounce torso to the left 8 times,
     flex feet, right arm in 3rd position

4   circle torso forwards then to the left
     and into neutral position

Exercise 5: "Breathings"

Terms

breathings	exercises which train conscious breathing
contract - release	tilting the pelvis backwards and forwards
high release	large back bend (arching)
lift	lifting the chest and the head (upwards lengthening)

Effect

This exercise promotes a fluent coordination of breathing with straightening and bending of the torso and with rotation of the spine. At the same time it provides opportunity for artistic and expressive posture work and arm gestures, all ensuing from the torso.

Level of difficulty

Grade 3 (for grade 1+2 in very simplified version, see Model Lesson 1+2)

Technical characteristics and execution

The complex sequences of movements which start in the pelvis and in the shoulder girdle are hard to describe and illustrate.

The starting position for these exercises is sitting cross-legged. The pelvis is tilted backwards (the body's centre of gravity is shifted backwards), the spine is rounded, the head is in the neutral position, and the arms rest slightly stretched on the knees. On inhalation, the torso, starting at the pelvis, is straightened up and tensed; on exhalation, the torso returns to its starting position. This basic exercise is varied by opening and *lifting* the chest and the head, and also by bringing the arms forwards into the V-position lifting them upwards and then dropping them into the neutral position. During this, the shoulder blades must be fixed downwards. To extend this exercise, a vertical rotation of the spine and the pelvis can be added. This is introduced by pulling back one shoulder (shoulder blade). The simultaneous extension and flexion of one leg, which starts in the forwards and backwards turn of the pelvis, is coordinated with the arm gestures. Smooth execution of the movements and a slow pace based on the breathing support this exercise.

Starting position: sitting cross-legged, back slightly rounded, arms on the knees, face forwards (Fig. 20.1).

cts. Sequence   Fig. 20.1-6

cts.	Sequence
4	straighten up torso while breathing in (Fig. 20.2)
4	back to starting position while breathing out
4	straighten up torso with *lift* of breast and head (Fig. 20.3)
4	starting position
4	straighten up torso with *lift* and arm movement (Fig. 20.4)
4	starting position
4	straighten up torso and rotate right side forwards, face to the right across the forward shoulder while breathing in (Fig. 20.5)
4	back to starting position while breathing out
4	straighten up torso and rotate left side forwards, face to the left across the forward shoulder
4	starting position
4	straighten up torso and rotate right side forwards, arm movement, face to the right over the forward shoulder (Fig. 20.6)
4	starting position
4	straighten up torso and rotate left side forwards, arm movement, face to the left over the forward shoulder
4	starting position

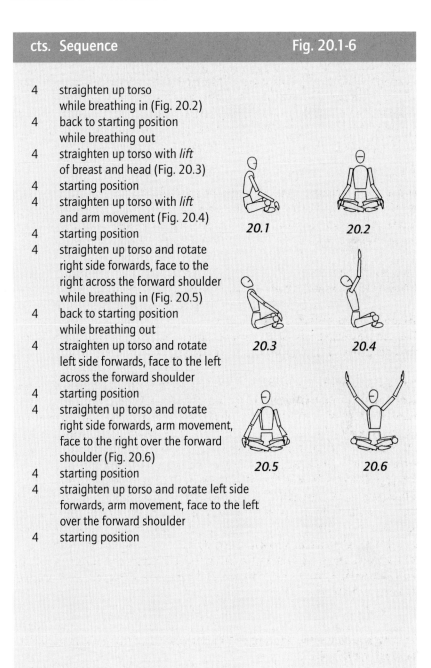

20.1   20.2   20.3   20.4   20.5   20.6

cts.	Sequence	Fig. 21.1-4
4	straighten up torso while rotating the right side forwards, simultaneous arm movement and *extension* of the right leg by rotating the right hip forwards, face to the right over the forward shoulder (Fig. 21.1)	*21.1*
1	rotate the torso with the left side forwards, through the turning of the right hip backwards the right leg is angled slightly, face to the left hand (Fig. 21.2)	*21.2*
1	rotate the torso with the left side backwards, through the accompanying turning of the left hip backwards the right leg bends a little further, continue to face to the left hand (Fig. 21.3)	*21.3*
1	rotate the torso with the right side backwards, face to the right hand	
1	actively lock right leg in, bend stretched torso forwards, open arms from inside to outside into 2nd position (Fig. 21.4).	*21.4*

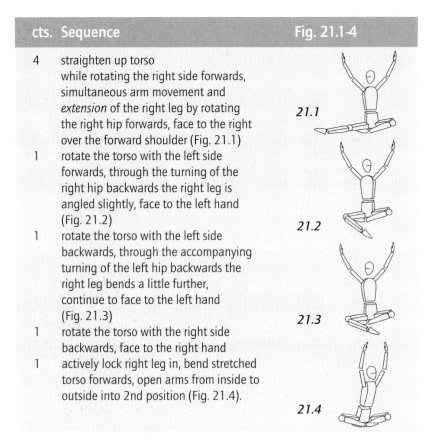

EXERCISE 6: "CHANGE LEGS"

In order to be able to start the whole sequence "Breathings" with the other side, a special way of changing legs is presented here.

Technical characteristics and execution
Changing legs from the right front side to the left front side when sitting cross-legged is coordinated with a movement of the arm and a rotation of the spine. The torso must be very straight. This produces a wide dance gesture. The precise technique was described in the "Breathings" exercise.

Starting position: sitting cross-legged, right leg to the front, arms in neutral position.

cts.	Sequence	Fig. 22.1-4
2	stretch the right leg by rotating the right side of the torso forwards, move arms to the right front up into 2nd position, face to the right (Fig. 22.1)	*22.1* 
2	stretch the left leg by rotating the left side of the torso forwards, move arms forwards to the left up into 2nd position, face to the left	
1	lock right leg in by rotating the left side of the torso backwards, move the right arm forwards, face to the right (Fig. 22.2)	*22.2* 
1	lock left leg in by rotating the right side of the torso backwards, move the left arm forwards, face to the left	
1	torso in neutral position, left arm in 3rd position (Fig. 22.3)	*22.3* 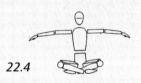
1	bend stretched torso forwards from the middle, open right arm from the inside into 2nd position, straighten torso (Fig. 22.4)	*22.4*

EXERCISE 7: "PLIÉS"

Terms

plié   bending the legs
flat back   bending the torso backwards while the back is stretched
lift   lifting the chest and the head

Effect

In this floor exercise the outward rotation of the hip – an essential aspect of *Jazz Dance* – and the coordination of bending and stretching the legs is practised. The exercise serves to prepare for *pliés and leg gestures* in statics and motion with associated smooth arm gestures, and rotation and tilting of the stretched torso to the side and forwards.

Level of difficulty
Grade 3 (for grade 1+2 in simplified version, see Model Lesson 1+2)

Technical characteristics and execution
Bending one leg in all its joints while simultaneously stretching the other one up to the tips of the toes is not a normal everyday form of coordination, but one very typical of dance. It must therefore be practised repeatedly through special exercises like the following.

The exercise is performed in the open sitting level. When the leg and foot joints are bent (*plié*), the heels stay on their points of contact with the floor and are only rolled about, i.e. they are not pulled towards the body. The body is upright.

At the beginning, the whole sequence should be executed with the legs in parallel position and without arm gestures or movements of the torso. When coordination of the arms is added, the head follows the arms, whose movement comes from the torso. The chest is *lifted*, the head moves diagonally upwards. When the chest is lifted, the head moves diagonally upwards.

Starting position: sitting with open legs (2nd position), arms in neutral position in front of the pelvis.

cts.	Sequence	Fig. 23.1-3

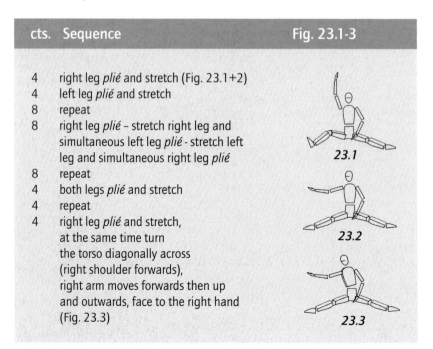

cts.	Sequence
4	right leg *plié* and stretch (Fig. 23.1+2)
4	left leg *plié* and stretch
8	repeat
8	right leg *plié* – stretch right leg and simultaneous left leg *plié* - stretch left leg and simultaneous right leg *plié*
8	repeat
4	both legs *plié* and stretch
4	repeat
4	right leg *plié* and stretch, at the same time turn the torso diagonally across (right shoulder forwards), right arm moves forwards then up and outwards, face to the right hand (Fig. 23.3)

23.1

23.2

23.3

cts.	Sequence (continued)	Fig. 23.4 - 6

4	left leg *plié* and stretch, at the same time turn the torso diagonally across (left shoulder forwards), left arm moves forwards then up and outwards, face to the left hand	**23.4**
8	repeat movements to the right and to the left	
16	8 times *plié* right and left alternating smoothly with arm movements and turns of the torso to the respective side, always face in the direction of the opening arm	
4	both legs *plié* and stretch, open both arms overhead, torso and face aligned to the front	**23.5**
4	repeat (Fig. 23.4)	
4	both legs *plié* and stretch, bend torso forwards with *flat back* starting at the centre, while stretching *lift*, arm movements see above (Fig. 23.5+6)	
4	repeat	**23.6**

EXERCISE 8: "FLEXIBILITY OF FEET AND LEGS"

Effect
Here the emphasis is on the mobilization of the leg and foot joints. By holding one leg just above the floor and performing fast leg changes with *lifted* head, the leg and stomach muscles are strengthened at the same time.

Level of difficulty
Grade 2 ↑
(for grade 1 in simplified version, see Model Lesson 1)

Technical characteristics and execution

By bending, stretching and circling, the leg and foot joints are mobilized in the lying level, with the torso firmly fixed in the neutral position. When rotating the free leg outwards, the pelvis is consciously fixed on the floor; when rotating it inwards, the shoulder and the arm of the opposite side are fixed on the floor. The lying leg (supporting leg) remains consciously stretched throughout the exercise, with advanced students holding it about five centimetres above the floor in order to strengthen it at the same time. In addition, the head and the shoulder girdle are *lifted* during the fast leg changes to fix the lumbar vertebrae on the floor.

Starting position: lying level, left leg stretched, right knee pulled against the breast with both hands (Fig. 24).

cts.	Sequence	Fig. 24+25

cts.	Sequence
8	8 foot circles outwards
8	8 foot circles inwards
4	pull knee outwards, fix left arm in 2nd position on the floor
4	pull knee against the breast and change hands
4	pull knee inwards, fix right arm in 2nd position on the floor
4	pull knee against the breast, hold with both hands
8	bounce knee 8 times towards the breast
2	put straight leg down next to left leg
2	bend left leg and pull against the breast
	repeat sequence with the left leg
16	pull right knee and left knee alternately against the breast 16 times and stretch again, *lifting* the head (Fig. 25)

Exercise 9: "Contractions"

Terms

contract - release	tilting the pelvis backwards and forwards by contracting and releasing
high release	large back stretch of torso
table top	torso is parallel with the floor

Effect

The main focus here is on developing *contraction* in connection with *relaxation* as a basic technique in *Jazz Dance* and *Modern Dance*. In addition, the flexibility of the hip joints and the lumbar vertebrae and the strength of the abdominals, the buttocks and the thigh muscles are trained. The basic form of this exercise is thus also an opportunity to work on the straightening of the pelvis. It is executed in all spatial planes in statics as well as in locomotion.

Level of difficulty

Grade 3 (for grade 1+2 in simplified version, see Model Lesson 1+2)

Technical characteristics and execution

Contraction here relates to the centre of the body (pelvic region) and is linked with a *release*. The pelvis is first tilted backwards by *contraction* of the abdominals and the buttocks (*contract*), the groin is stretched and lengthened, shoulder and hip joints stay above each other in a single line. By releasing the *contraction* and bending the hip joint, the pelvis tilts forwards again and the lumbar vertebrae moves back into its physiological lordosis (*release*). *High release* induces an overstretching of the whole spine and the hip joints.

This basic exercise is first executed in the knee sit and, as the level advances, in the knee stand. The exercises are rendered more difficult through variations with fast changes of the torso position, so that the body is prepared for the much more complicated techniques in stand and locomotion.

Starting position: knee sit with straight torso, arms in neutral position.

cts. Sequence   Fig. 26.1-3

4   *contract – release* (Fig. 26.1+2)
4   repeat
4   lower torso to *table top* position,
      balance on the knees (Fig. 26.3)

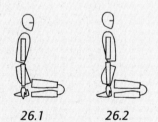

26.1   *26.2*

26.3

cts. Sequence (continued)   Fig. 26.4-6+27.1+2

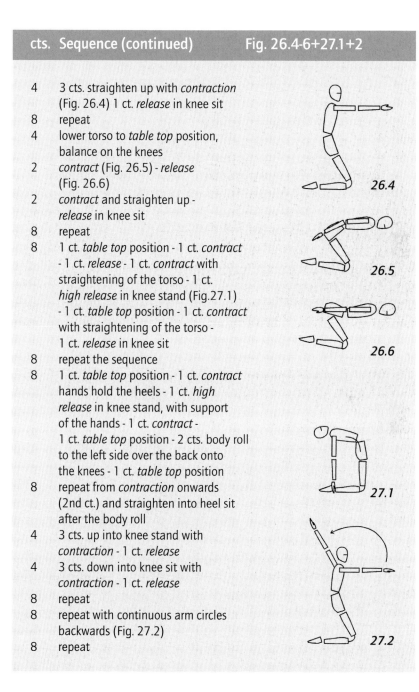

4	3 cts. straighten up with *contraction* (Fig. 26.4) 1 ct. *release* in knee sit
8	repeat
4	lower torso to *table top* position, balance on the knees
2	*contract* (Fig. 26.5) - *release* (Fig. 26.6)
2	*contract* and straighten up - *release* in knee sit
8	repeat
8	1 ct. *table top* position - 1 ct. *contract* - 1 ct. *release* - 1 ct. *contract* with straightening of the torso - 1 ct. *high release* in knee stand (Fig.27.1) - 1 ct. *table top* position - 1 ct. *contract* with straightening of the torso - 1 ct. *release* in knee sit
8	repeat the sequence
8	1 ct. *table top* position - 1 ct. *contract* hands hold the heels - 1 ct. *high release* in knee stand, with support of the hands - 1 ct. *contract* - 1 ct. *table top* position - 2 cts. body roll to the left side over the back onto the knees - 1 ct. *table top* position
8	repeat from *contraction* onwards (2nd ct.) and straighten into heel sit after the body roll
4	3 cts. up into knee stand with *contraction* - 1 ct. *release*
4	3 cts. down into knee sit with *contraction* - 1 ct. *release*
8	repeat
8	repeat with continuous arm circles backwards (Fig. 27.2)
8	repeat

26.4

26.5

26.6

27.1

27.2

3.4.3 Centre Work 2

EXERCISE 10: "BOUNCING PLIÉS"

Terms
bouncing pliés   bending the legs and bouncing

Effect
Mobilization of the leg joints in parallel and turned out positions through fast, deep bounces as preparation for *pliés*.

Level of difficulty
Grade 3 ↑ (for grade 1+2 at the barre, see Model Lesson 1+2)

Technical characteristics and execution
Bouncing pliés are deep leg bounces executed in the 1st and 2nd position parallel and turned out. The torso remains straight and is well tensed (no shifting backwards with the pelvis). The knees are bounced over the toes along the axis, the heels stay on the floor and the weight is distributed evenly on both feet, with the plantar arches straightened up.

Starting position: 1st position parallel, arms in neutral position.

cts.	Sequence	Fig. 28
8	16 fast *pliés*	
8	repeat in 1st position turned out	
8	repeat in 2nd position parallel	
8	repeat in 2nd position turned out (Fig. 28)	

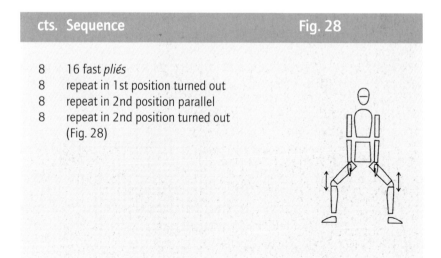

EXERCISE 11: "PLIÉS"

Terms

demi plié	small bend of the knees
grand plié	deep bend of the knees
relevé	lifting into the ball and toe stand
tendu	brushing out the stretched leg

Effect

Development of the pliés as an important and fundamental dancing technique: the muscles of the leg and the hip and the joints are optimally warmed-up, lengthened and strengthened. The interplay of the joints in parallel, turned out and turned in positions is developed. The pliés help to build up a correct posture and develop confidence in letting the body move upwards and downwards at the same time. With more complex exercises, as described below, various ways of placing and directing the arms precisely are learnt, and the ability to coordinate movements is developed. Connecting pliés with relevés and head isolations aims at training balance.

Level of difficulty

Grade 3 ↑ (for grade 1+2 in simplified version at the barre, see Model Lesson 1+2).

Technical characteristics and execution

The pliés are a fundamental technique for the dancer. In connection with relevés, they are a good way of preparing for taking off into fast vigorous jumps and for levelling off the jump elastically. To be able to execute pliés with precision, it is essential to learn to coordinate the bend of the joints along the axis with slow continuous execution (see also section 3.1.4). and to stabilize the entire torso in the vertical position. It is important to imagine that one is lowering oneself downwards towards the floor and at the same time moving towards the ceiling. In Jazz Dance and Modern Dance all positions, turned out, parallel, and turned in, are considered.

Demi plié: maximal bending of the leg joints with the weight on the whole foot sole with well raised plantar arches and perpendicularly tensed torso posture. The heels must stay on the floor (building up a maximum of pre-tension, for example for take off), with the pelvis optimally aligned. After reaching the lowest point, the stretching phase of the legs is started without interruption of the flow of the movement.

Grand (deep) plié: after achieving the position of the demi plié, the legs are bent, the heels are lifted from the floor, while the torso and the pelvis remain aligned. Braking power, conscious bending of the joints and upwards stretch tension of the torso should be used to prevent the heels from coming down. When the lowest point is reached, the stretching phase of the legs is started, without interruption of the flow of the movement, by pressing the heels back into the floor. To open the legs from the hips in turned out positions, the knees are actively thrust outwards over the feet and the pelvis is thrust forwards.

Relevé: by pulling the weight of the body upwards it is *lifted* into the ball stand or the high toe stand. The weight must be distributed on all toes, the ankle joints must not bend outwards or inwards, the whole body is highly tensed and stretched. The *relevé* can also be done explosively, for example in preparation for jumps or when taking off for turns. Lowering down from the *relevé* should be performed slowly using braking power and stretch tension upwards.

Starting position: 1st position turned out, arms in neutral position.

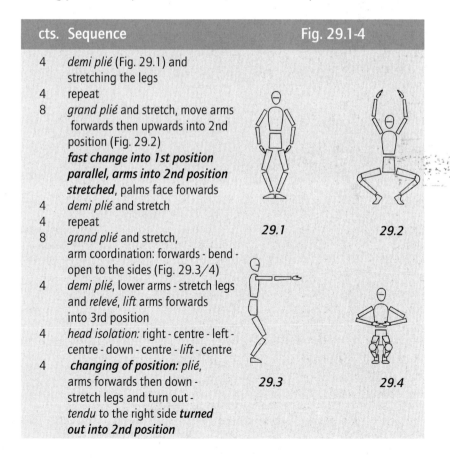

cts.	Sequence	Fig. 29.1-4
4	*demi plié* (Fig. 29.1) and stretching the legs	
4	repeat	
8	*grand plié* and stretch, move arms forwards then upwards into 2nd position (Fig. 29.2) **fast change into 1st position parallel, arms into 2nd position stretched**, palms face forwards	
4	*demi plié* and stretch	
4	repeat	
8	*grand plié* and stretch, arm coordination: forwards - bend - open to the sides (Fig. 29.3/4)	
4	*demi plié*, lower arms - stretch legs and *relevé*, *lift* arms forwards into 3rd position	
4	*head isolation:* right - centre - left - centre - down - centre - *lift* - centre	
4	**changing of position:** *plié*, arms forwards then down - stretch legs and turn out - *tendu* to the right side **turned out into 2nd position**	

29.1

29.2

29.3

29.4

cts.	Sequence (continued)	Fig.30.1-5

4   *demi plié* and stretch (Fig. 30.1)
4   repeat
8   *grand plié* and stretch,
     move arms forwards then upwards
     into 2nd position (Fig. 30.2)
     **fast change into 2nd position
     parallel, arms stretched in 2nd position**,   **30.1**
     palms face forwards
4   *demi plié* and stretch
4   repeat
8   *grand plié* and stretch,
     arm coordination: stretched forwards
     - bend - forwards - open to the sides
4   *demi plié*, arms down - stretch legs
     and *relevé, lift* arms forwards then   **30.2**
     into 3rd position
4   *head isolation*: right - centre - left -
     centre - down - centre - *lift* - centre
     (Fig. 30.3)
4   **change of position:** *plié*, arms forwards
     then down - stretch legs and turn out -
     tendu forwards to the right side
     turned out into 4th position   **30.3**
4   *demi plié* and stretch (Fig. 30.4)
4   repeat
8   *grand plié*, arm coordination:
     stretched forwards - bend - forwards
     - open to the sides
     fast change to the 4th position parallel,
     arms stretched in 2nd position,   **30.4**
     palms face forwards
4   *demi plié* and stretch (Fig. 30.5)
4   repeat
8   *grand plié*, arm coordination:
     stretched forwards - bend - forwards
     - open to the sides

     30.5

cts. Sequence (continued)   Fig.30.6

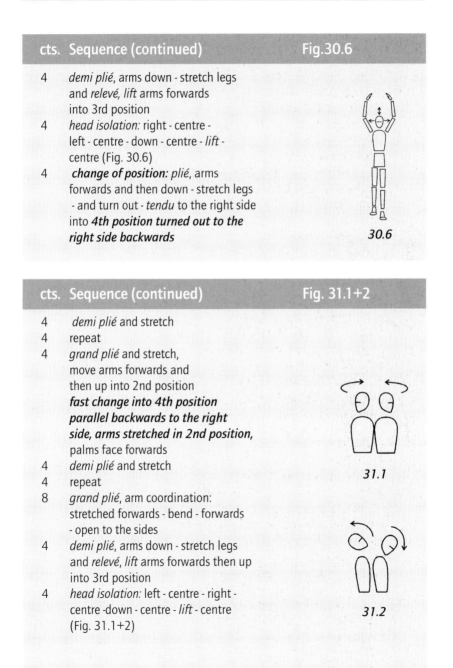

4   *demi plié*, arms down - stretch legs
    and *relevé, lift* arms forwards
    into 3rd position
4   *head isolation:* right - centre -
    left - centre - down - centre - *lift* -
    centre (Fig. 30.6)
4   **change of position:** *plié*, arms
    forwards and then down - stretch legs
    - and turn out - *tendu* to the right side
    into **4th position turned out to the
    right side backwards**

30.6

cts. Sequence (continued)   Fig. 31.1+2

4   *demi plié* and stretch
4   repeat
4   *grand plié* and stretch,
    move arms forwards and
    then up into 2nd position
    **fast change into 4th position
    parallel backwards to the right
    side, arms stretched in 2nd position,**
    palms face forwards
4   *demi plié* and stretch
4   repeat
8   *grand plié*, arm coordination:
    stretched forwards - bend - forwards
    - open to the sides
4   *demi plié*, arms down - stretch legs
    and *relevé, lift* arms forwards then up
    into 3rd position
4   *head isolation:* left - centre - right -
    centre -down - centre - *lift* - centre
    (Fig. 31.1+2)

31.1

31.2

cts.	Sequence (continued)	Fig. 31.3

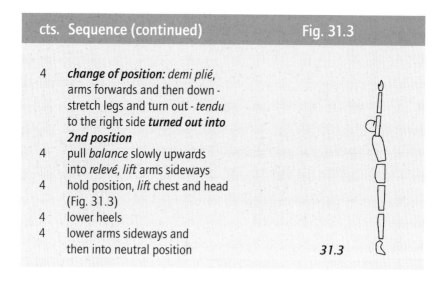

4	*change of position: demi plié,* arms forwards and then down - stretch legs and turn out - *tendu* to the right side **turned out into 2nd position**	
4	pull *balance* slowly upwards into *relevé*, *lift* arms sideways	
4	hold position, *lift* chest and head (Fig. 31.3)	
4	lower heels	
4	lower arms sideways and then into neutral position	*31.3*

EXERCISE 12: "LEG – ARM – COORDINATIONS"

Effect

The ability to change tension quickly and to coordinate leg and arm movements in the most different positions and rhythmical sequences is trained in this exercise.

Level of difficulty

Grade 3 ↑ (for grade 2 in simplified version, see Model Lesson 2)

Technical characteristics and execution

Stylistic *Jazz Dance* elements are incorporated in this exercise. The *plié – relevé* positions and inwardly rotated leg positions in connection with jazz arms are typical coordination exercises in preparation for *Jazz Dance*. Each position should be practised distinctly and with accentuation.

In addition, fast changes between *contraction* and *release* are typical, as the arm movement at the end of the exercise demonstrates. Here, as the torso is straightened fast and overstretches into *high release*, the arms are thrust upwards, dropped and swung crossed around the body. Then they are fixed in the 2nd position while the legs are simultaneously stretched and rotated outwards and the torso aligned.

Starting position: 2nd position turned out, arms in 2nd position.

cts.	Sequence	Fig. 32.1-8

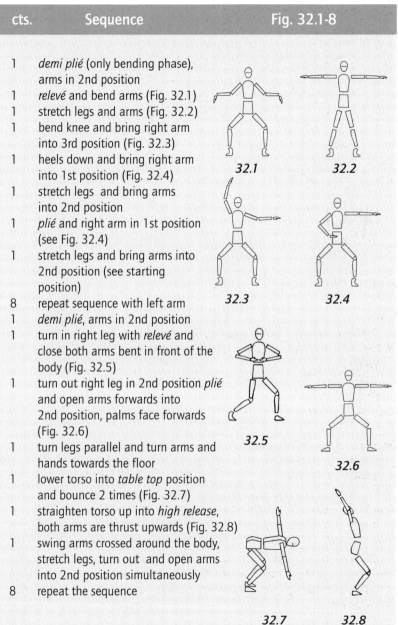

1	*demi plié* (only bending phase), arms in 2nd position	
1	*relevé* and bend arms (Fig. 32.1)	
1	stretch legs and arms (Fig. 32.2)	
1	bend knee and bring right arm into 3rd position (Fig. 32.3)	
1	heels down and bring right arm into 1st position (Fig. 32.4)	
1	stretch legs and bring arms into 2nd position	
1	*plié* and right arm in 1st position (see Fig. 32.4)	
1	stretch legs and bring arms into 2nd position (see starting position)	
8	repeat sequence with left arm	
1	*demi plié*, arms in 2nd position	
1	turn in right leg with *relevé* and close both arms bent in front of the body (Fig. 32.5)	
1	turn out right leg in 2nd position *plié* and open arms forwards into 2nd position, palms face forwards (Fig. 32.6)	
1	turn legs parallel and turn arms and hands towards the floor	
1	lower torso into *table top* position and bounce 2 times (Fig. 32.7)	
1	straighten torso up into *high release*, both arms are thrust upwards (Fig. 32.8)	
1	swing arms crossed around the body, stretch legs, turn out and open arms into 2nd position simultaneously	
8	repeat the sequence	

32.1   *32.2*

32.3   *32.4*

32.5

32.6

32.7   *32.8*

EXERCISE 13: "FLEX-POINTS AND TURNS"

Terms

flex-points	bending and stretching movements in the foot and knee joint
en dehors	direction of turn away from supporting leg, outwards
tendu	brushes
legato	smooth, connected (musical term)

Effect

This exercise develops the fast and exact bend-stretch-coordination of the knee and the foot joint. It improves the standing stability on one leg and prepares for turns.

Level of difficulty

Grade 3 ↑

Technical characteristics and execution

Flex-points are fast bending and stretching movements in the knee and foot joint of the free leg with the thigh fixed and rotated out. The flexed foot is brought alternatingly next to the back of the ankle of the supporting leg or the pointed foot is brought next to the front of it, or vice versa. Between these movements the leg is briefly stretched sideways. The foot joint is bent or stretched at the turning point of the stretching movement. In order to keep long term balance on the supporting leg while the free leg moves swiftly, it is necessary to fix the hip of the free leg with the help of the abductors and the outward rotators of the thigh, and to tense the whole torso upwards.

This ability to maintain balance is necessary for the following *turns* (see section 3.2.5). To train orientation by means of the head, precise take off for the *turn* starting from the 4th position *plié* (rear leg stretched), support work with the arms (open and close) and safe landing in the new direction, after the preparatory phase for the take off, quarter *turns* should be practised first, followed by half *turns* and finally full *turns en dehors* (direction of the *turn* away from the supporting leg, outwards).

Starting position: stand on left leg, right leg *tendu* side, arms in 2nd position.

cts. Sequence	Fig. 33.1-6

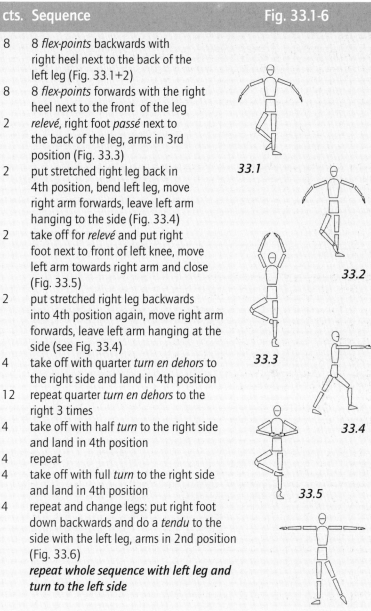

8   8 *flex-points* backwards with right heel next to the back of the left leg (Fig. 33.1+2)

8   8 *flex-points* forwards with the right heel next to the front of the leg

2   *relevé*, right foot *passé* next to the back of the leg, arms in 3rd position (Fig. 33.3)

2   put stretched right leg back in 4th position, bend left leg, move right arm forwards, leave left arm hanging to the side (Fig. 33.4)

2   take off for *relevé* and put right foot next to front of left knee, move left arm towards right arm and close (Fig. 33.5)

2   put stretched right leg backwards into 4th position again, move right arm forwards, leave left arm hanging at the side (see Fig. 33.4)

4   take off with quarter *turn en dehors* to the right side and land in 4th position

12   repeat quarter *turn en dehors* to the right 3 times

4   take off with half *turn* to the right side and land in 4th position

4   repeat

4   take off with full *turn* to the right side and land in 4th position

4   repeat and change legs: put right foot down backwards and do a *tendu* to the side with the left leg, arms in 2nd position (Fig. 33.6)

repeat whole sequence with left leg and turn to the left side

33.1

33.2

33.3

33.4

33.5

33.6

Variation 1

cts.	Sequence
2	2 *flex-points* with the front of the right foot put next to the leg
2	4 *flex-points* with the front of the right foot put next to the leg at double speed
4	repeat
2	2 *flex-points* with the front of the right foot put next to the leg
2	4 *flex-points* with the front of the right foot put next to the leg at double speed
4	*relevé* and 4th position
4	double *turn en dehors* to the right side and change legs
20	repeat sequence with the other leg

Variation 2

cts.	Sequence
4	4 *flex-points* to the right side backwards forwards coordinated with a *legato* arm circle inwards
4	4 *flex-points* to the right side forwards backwards coordinated with a *legato* arm circle outwards
	repeat sequence with the other leg
	advanced students can practise the variations in relevé

Exercise 14: "Leg Swings and Laterals"

Terms
laterals   bending the torso sideways

Effect
Improvement of the active flexibility of the hip joints and extended lengthening of the spine sideways in the frontal plane of motion. In addition, the lateral abdominals are strengthened by accelerating the pace and by requiring a higher number of exercises within one sequence.

Level of difficulty
Grade 3 ↑ (for grade 1+2 in simplified version at the barre, see Model Lesson 1+2)

Technical characteristics and execution

During *leg swings*, the foot brushes through the 1st position, and the bent leg swings in an outward rotation (*attitude*) forwards and then sideways. The torso and the pelvis remain fixed in neutral position, while the *laterals*, the lateral flexion of the spine, are activated by a side shift of the hips. Movement must be restricted to the frontal plane and a hollow back avoided. These exercises are at first executed slowly and under control. Then they become gradually faster and the number of repetitions is increased.

Starting position: stand on turned out left leg, right leg *tendu* sideways, arms in 2nd position.

cts.	Sequence	Fig. 34.1-6
4	bent right leg swings turned out through 1st position forwards-sideways-forwards-sideways (Fig. 34.1+2), integrate shift of weight over 2nd position *plié*	
4	bent left leg swings turned out through 1st position forwards-sideways-forwards-sideways, integrated shift of weight see above	
4	bent right leg swings turned out forwards-sideways-forwards-sideways	
4	3 cts. balance in *relevé* on the left leg, arms in V-position, then put weight onto both legs in 2nd position (Fig. 34.3+4)	
4	shift hip to the left side, lateral flexion to the right side and back into neutral position (Fig. 34.5+6)	
4	shift hip to the right side, lateral flexion to the left side and back into neutral position	
8	repeat the *laterals* for the other side (Fig. 34.5+6)	
16	repeat the *leg swings* starting with the left leg with balance on the right leg	
12	do 6 *laterals* at double speed (Fig. 34.5+6)	
4	lower the arms	

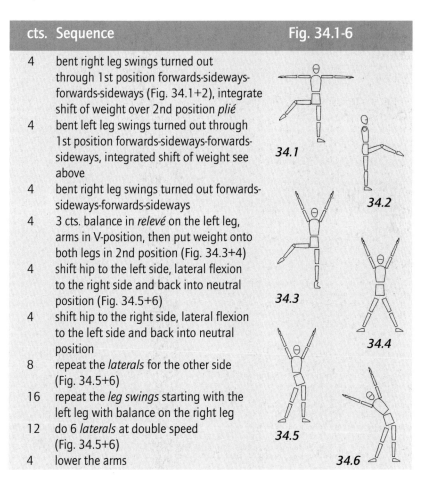

34.1
34.2
34.3
34.4
34.5
34.6

EXERCISE 15: "LATERALS, FLAT BACK AND HORIZONTAL SWINGS"

Terms

laterals	bending the torso to the side (lateral flexion)
flat back	bending the torso with stretched back
horizontal swings	swinging the torso in *flat back* position from one side to the other

Effect
Same as Exercise 14 with even greater strengthening of all the muscles of the torso.

Level of difficulty
Grade 3 ↑ (for grade 1+2 in simplified version, see Model Lesson 1+2)

Technical characteristics and execution
Variation of the previous exercise. Starting with the lateral flexion the torso is turned diagonally forwards to *flat back* position. It is then swung to the other side on the horizontal plane. Starting from the pelvis, it is turned back into the frontal plane to the position of lateral flexion and finally brought back into neutral position. Wide torso movements, precise positions without making a hollow back and fixation of the arms in a downwards pulled shoulder girdle demand a lot with regard to torso strength and flexibility. Possible variations for advanced students are rotations into *flat back back bend* and *release swings* (cf. **Centre Work** 3).

Starting position: stand in 2nd position parallel, arms in V-position.

cts.	Sequence	Fig. 35.1-4
2	hip shift to the left side and lateral flexion to the right side (Fig. 35.1)	
2	rotate the torso to the *flat back* position diagonally to the right side (Fig. 35.2)	
2	swing torso horizontally to the left side (Fig. 35.3)	*35.1* *35.2*
2	rotate the torso for lateral flexion to the left side (Fig. 35.4)	
2	straighten up into neutral position	
10	repeat whole sequence for the other side	*35.3* *35.4*

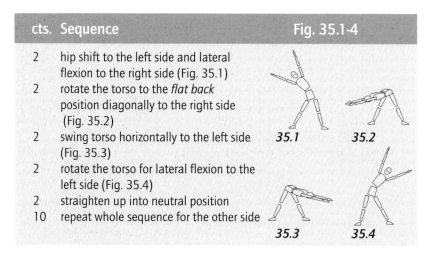

Exercise 16: "Leg Stretching in Lunge Position"

Effect
Expansion of the amplitude of mobility of the legs. Through passive-static and passive-dynamic exercises, the hip joint flexors, the hip joint extensors, the adductors and the rear muscles of the lower leg are lengthened.

Level of difficulty
Grade 3 ↑ (for grade 1+2 in simplified version, see Model Lesson 1+2)

Technical characteristics and execution
Lengthening in various *lunge* positions typically involves exercises in which lengthening is stimulated through body weight, through active pulls and through soft bounces around the point of tension. The level of difficulty and the effectiveness of these exercises are gradually increased through deeper and greater lunges and through flex positions of the feet and bending of the torso. It is important to ensure that the perpendicular positions of the joints are maintained, that the weight is placed properly over the feet and the toes, and that the position of the pelvis is absolutely correct for each particular plane of movement. Changes of direction and lordosis must be avoided.

Starting position: the feet are parallel, the weight is on the forward right foot and on the balls of the left foot, the arms are in 2nd *jazz* position.

cts.	Sequence	Fig. 36.1-2
6	bounce left heel to the ground 6 times, bend and stretch right knee simultaneously, leave left leg straight (Fig. 36.1+2)	
2	change legs: bring left knee forwards and *lift* up (Fig. 36.3) - put foot down next to right leg - *lift* right knee up - put right foot down backwards onto ball	

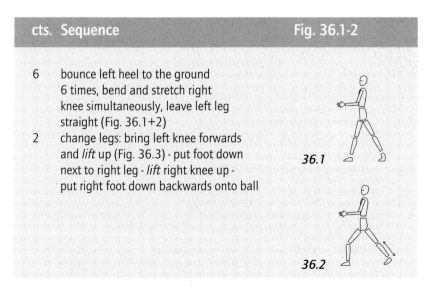

36.1

36.2

cts.	Sequence (continued)	Fig. 36.3-7
8	repeat for the other side ***change of positions*** (keeping time): left foot slides out backwards into a deep *lunge* position, the right bent leg is turned out, hands support to the left and right of the knee (Fig. 36.4)	
8	8 bounces of the pelvis forwards- downwards with simultaneous pull of the left heel backwards	*36.3*
4	change legs: in deep *plié* put left foot next to right foot (Fig. 36.5) - right foot slides out backwards until leg is straight	
8	repeat for the other side	
4	change legs, see above (cf. Fig. 36.5)	*36.4*
4	4 bounces of the pelvis forwards- downwards with simultaneous pull of the left heel backwards	
8	stretch right leg and bring torso next to right leg, starting from the sternum, hold lengthening position (Fig. 36.6)	*36.5*
4	bend right leg again and bounce pelvis 4 times forwards-downwards, pull left heel backwards simultaneously	
8	stretch right leg and bring torso to the right leg, starting from the sternum, hold lengthening position (cf. Fig. 36.6)	
4	change legs, see above (cf. Fig. 36.5)	*36.6*
24	repeat with other leg forward	
8	run forwards on hands for 4 cts. until torso is straight parallel to the floor - hold for 4 cts. (Fig. 36.7)	
4	change legs, see above (cf. Fig. 36.5)	
12	repeat for the other side	*36.7*

Starting position: standing, the feet are parallel and closed, the arms are in 3rd position.

cts.	Sequence	Fig. 37.1+2

8	1 ct. right leg slides forwards parallel to position of feet - 7 cts. lower torso with *flat back* onto front leg, hands support next to foot (Fig. 37.1)	
8	flex and roll down right foot 4 times (Fig. 37.2)	
8	7 cts. *lift* torso with *flat back* - 1 ct. brush right foot in	
24	repeat for the other side	

Exercise 17: "Leg Fortification and Balance"

Terms
relevé   *lift* into ball and toe stand

Effect
As the name implies, this exercise develops sense of balance in *relevé* positions and the strength of the leg muscles.

Level of difficulty
Grade 3 ↑ (for grade 1+2 in simplified version at the barre, see Model Lesson 1+2)

Technical characteristics and execution
In *lunge* position forwards and sidewards, very slow *relevés* and knee bounces are executed. The torso is stabilized in the upright position with the same posture criteria as described in Exercise 16.

Starting position: standing, 2nd position turned out, the arms are in 2nd position.

cts.	Sequence	Fig. 38.1-4
8	4 cts. bend right leg (*lunge* side) 4 knee bounces (Fig. 38.1)	
8	4 cts. right foot *relevé* - 4 bounces (Fig. 38.2)	
8	4 cts. quarter *turn* to the right into *lunge* forwards. Arms extended in front position - 4 knee bounces (Fig. 38.3)	
8	4 cts. left foot *relevé* - 4 knee bounces (Fig. 38.4)	
8	4 cts. roll left foot down - 4 knee bounces	
8	4 cts. quarter *turn* to the left while facing forwards again, arms in 2nd position - 4 knee bounces (cf. Fig. 38.2)	
8	4 cts. roll down right foot - 4 knee bounces (cf. Fig. 38.1)	
4	stretch right leg *repeat whole sequence for the other side*	

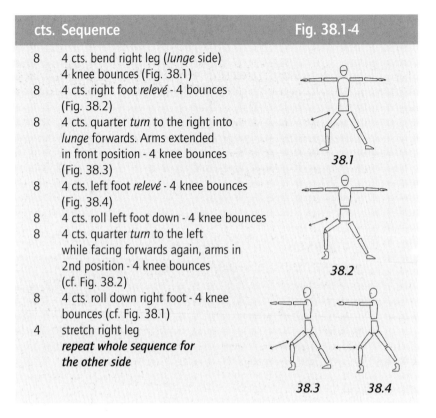

38.1

38.2

38.3   *38.4*

EXERCISE 18: "LEG STRETCHING AND FLAT BACK"

Effect
Lengthening of the extensors and the adductors of the hip joint and strengthening of the back extensors.

Level of difficulty
Grade 2 ↑

Technical characteristics and execution
In this mobility exercise, in the 2nd position parallel and in a *lunge* position sidewards with *flat back* of the torso forwards, the muscles of the back are strengthened simultaneously. All technical characteristics have already been described above.

Starting position: standing, large 2nd position parallel, the arms are in 2nd position.

cts.	Sequence	Fig. 39.1-3
4	bounce torso 4 times deeply with *flat back* (Fig. 39.1)	
4	bounce torso 4 times deeply with *flat back* in *plié* (Fig. 39.2)	
4	bounce torso 4 times deeply with *flat back*	
4	bounce torso 4 times deeply with *flat back* in *plié*	
4	bend right leg (Fig. 39.3)	
4	bounce 4 times in right knee	
4	shift weight over both legs with *plié* and bend left leg	
4	bounce knee 4 times	
16	repeat right and left	
4	shift weight in *plié* into centre	
4	bounce torso 4 times deeply in *plié* (cf. Fig. 39.2)	
4	bounce torso 4 times deeply with straight legs (cf. Fig. 39.1)	
4	stretch and straighten torso up	

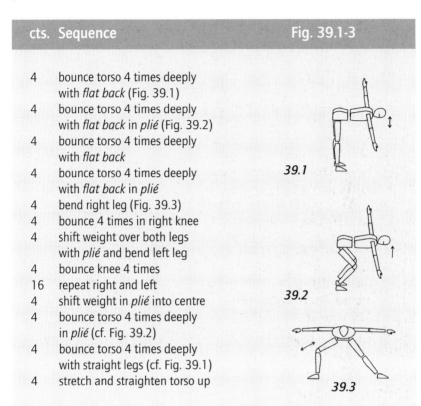

39.1

39.2

39.3

3.4.4 Barre

The barre provides balance support, and should therefore be used at beginner levels (see Model Lesson 1+2) and during preparation of more complex techniques. It is also very suitable for passive lengthening exercises with large amplitudes of movement of the torso and the legs. Many exercise sequences are similar to the ones executed in free standing, except that now one leg rests on the barre, and the scope of movement in the hip joint is thus greater. All movements are first executed slowly and continuously. This prepares the body for great amplitudes of movement and allows effective monitoring and correction work.

When working at the barre, the following basic positions must be observed:

1. *Front towards the barre* (side position): the hands, spread to shoulder width, rest lightly on the barre, not "holding tight". The body faces the barre, one forearm's length away from it, the head is upright, the eyes look straight ahead, the shoulders are pulled down.

2. *Profile towards the barre* (parallel position): one hand rests lightly on the barre, the upper arm is vertical next to the body, the lower arm is extended diagonally forwards. Good alignment, shoulder girdle and pelvic girdle make one front, eyes look straight ahead.

EXERCISE 19: "FLAT BACKS AND CONTRACTION"

Effect
Lengthening of the muscles of the shoulder girdle and the rear leg. Development of *contraction* with the torso in *table top* position.

Level of difficulty
Grade 2 ↑ (for grade 1 in simplified version, see Model Lesson 1)

Technical characteristics and execution
With the torso in *table top* position and hands at shoulder width holding the barre, the weight is slowly shifted forwards and backwards. The elbows, kept parallel, are shifted downwards underneath the shoulder girdle until the torso "hangs" in the bent arms. The heels remain on the ground, achieving a simultaneous lengthening of the calf muscles. The *contractions in table top* position are restricted to the pelvic region, the buttocks are consciously contracted and released, the upper torso remains completely still and straight.

Starting position: standing facing the barre, 2nd position parallel, hands rest on the barre at shoulder width, torso and legs are at an angle of 90 degrees (Fig. 40.1).

cts.	Sequence	Fig. 43.1-4

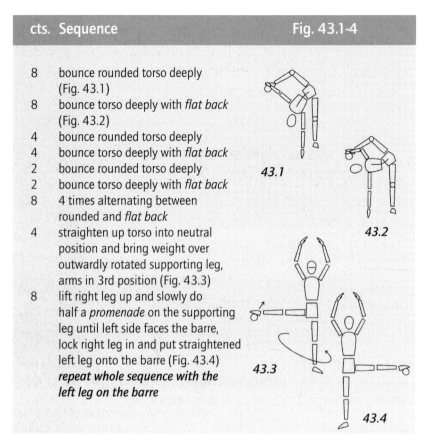

8	bounce rounded torso deeply (Fig. 43.1)
8	bounce torso deeply with *flat back* (Fig. 43.2)
4	bounce rounded torso deeply
4	bounce torso deeply with *flat back*
2	bounce rounded torso deeply
2	bounce torso deeply with *flat back*
8	4 times alternating between rounded and *flat back*
4	straighten up torso into neutral position and bring weight over outwardly rotated supporting leg, arms in 3rd position (Fig. 43.3)
8	lift right leg up and slowly do half a *promenade* on the supporting leg until left side faces the barre, lock right leg in and put straightened left leg onto the barre (Fig. 43.4) ***repeat whole sequence with the left leg on the barre***

43.1

43.2

43.3

43.4

Exercise 22: "Leg and Torso Stretching"

Terms

| *flat back back bend* | bend the torso backwards with straight back |

Effect
Extensive lengthening of the legs and the spine in and through all planes of movement.

Level of difficulty
Grade 2 ↑ (for grade 1 in simplified version, see Model Lesson 1)

When working at the barre, the following basic positions must be observed:

1. *Front towards the barre* (side position): the hands, spread to shoulder width, rest lightly on the barre, not "holding tight". The body faces the barre, one forearm's length away from it, the head is upright, the eyes look straight ahead, the shoulders are pulled down.

2. *Profile towards the barre* (parallel position): one hand rests lightly on the barre, the upper arm is vertical next to the body, the lower arm is extended diagonally forwards. Good alignment, shoulder girdle and pelvic girdle make one front, eyes look straight ahead.

EXERCISE 19: "FLAT BACKS AND CONTRACTION"

Effect
Lengthening of the muscles of the shoulder girdle and the rear leg. Development of *contraction* with the torso in *table top* position.

Level of difficulty
Grade 2 ↑ (for grade 1 in simplified version, see Model Lesson 1)

Technical characteristics and execution
With the torso in *table top* position and hands at shoulder width holding the barre, the weight is slowly shifted forwards and backwards. The elbows, kept parallel, are shifted downwards underneath the shoulder girdle until the torso "hangs" in the bent arms. The heels remain on the ground, achieving a simultaneous lengthening of the calf muscles. The *contractions in table top* position are restricted to the pelvic region, the buttocks are consciously contracted and released, the upper torso remains completely still and straight.

Starting position: standing facing the barre, 2nd position parallel, hands rest on the barre at shoulder width, torso and legs are at an angle of 90 degrees (Fig. 40.1).

cts.	Sequence	Fig. 40.1-4
4	shift straightened torso forwards until elbows are underneath shoulder girdle, head is underneath the barre (Fig. 40.2)	
4	back to starting position	
8	bounce torso deeply, hands touch the barre with the side of the little finger	
16	repeat	
8	shift torso forwards and backwards (see above)	
8	4 times *contract - release* (Fig. 40.3+4)	
16	repeat	

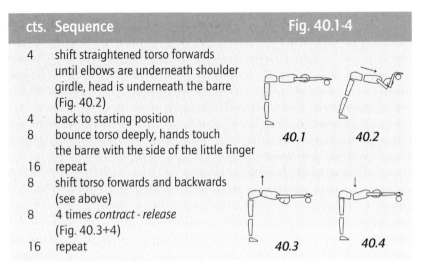

40.1   40.2

40.3   40.4

EXERCISE 20: "LEG STRETCHING"

Effect
Lengthening of the hip and leg muscles at the front and at the back.

Level of difficulty
Grade 2 ↑ (for grade 1 in simplified version, see Model Lesson 1)

Technical characteristics and execution
As with all lengthening exercises, it is essential to work in functionally correct body positions. In this exercise, the heel of the supporting leg remains fixed on the floor, the pelvis is always parallel to the barre.

Starting position: standing facing the barre, legs are parallel, right arch of the foot rests on the barre with the knee bent, hands rest next to it, torso is upright (Fig. 41.1).

cts.	Sequence	Fig. 41.1+2
4	stretch right leg, torso lies rounded on the leg (Fig. 41.2)	
4	bend right leg and starting position	
8	repeat	

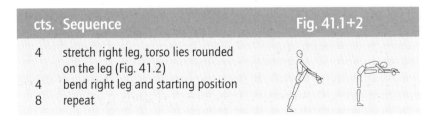

cts. Sequence	Fig. 42

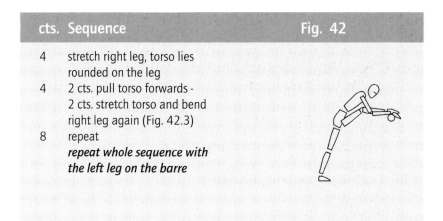

4	stretch right leg, torso lies rounded on the leg
4	2 cts. pull torso forwards - 2 cts. stretch torso and bend right leg again (Fig. 42.3)
8	repeat
	repeat whole sequence with the left leg on the barre

EXERCISE 21: "BEND AND BOUNCE"

Terms
promenade   turning on the supporting leg through repeated shifts forwards of the heel

Effect
Lengthening of the legs and strengthening of the back muscles. Perpendicular balancing and fixation of the body over the supporting leg.

Level of difficulty
Grade 2 ↑ (for grade 1 in simplified version, see Model Lesson 1)

Technical characteristics and execution
As far as torso work is concerned, this exercise corresponds to the "BEND AND BOUNCE" exercise described at the very start of the catalogue of exercises. Here, it is modified by putting one leg sideways onto the barre, so that the bounces are now accomplished in a very wide 2nd position. Since the weight of the body is supported by the arch on the barre, it must be brought back over the supporting leg using the abductors before the leg is *lifted* off the barre. This whole procedure adds to the level of difficulty.

Starting position: right side towards the barre, right leg lies bent on the barre, arch supports, right hand holds the barre in front of the right foot.

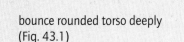

cts.	Sequence	Fig. 43.1-4

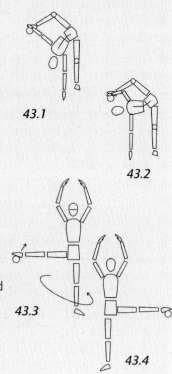

8	bounce rounded torso deeply (Fig. 43.1)
8	bounce torso deeply with *flat back* (Fig. 43.2)
4	bounce rounded torso deeply
4	bounce torso deeply with *flat back*
2	bounce rounded torso deeply
2	bounce torso deeply with *flat back*
8	4 times alternating between rounded and *flat back*
4	straighten up torso into neutral position and bring weight over outwardly rotated supporting leg, arms in 3rd position (Fig. 43.3)
8	lift right leg up and slowly do half a *promenade* on the supporting leg until left side faces the barre, lock right leg in and put straightened left leg onto the barre (Fig. 43.4) *repeat whole sequence with the left leg on the barre*

43.1

43.2

43.3

43.4

Exercise 22: "Leg and Torso Stretching"

Terms

flat back back bend   bend the torso backwards with straight back

Effect

Extensive lengthening of the legs and the spine in and through all planes of movement.

Level of difficulty

Grade 2 ↑ (for grade 1 in simplified version, see Model Lesson 1)

Technical characteristics and execution

When changing planes of movement, it is essential to ensure that the positions of the pelvis and the legs are also turned precisely and that the arms remain fixed. The torso is stretched upwards before each movement.

Starting position: right side to the barre, right leg lies straightened on the barre, arch is on the barre, both legs are turned out, arms in V-position.

cts.	Sequence	Fig. 44.1-6
		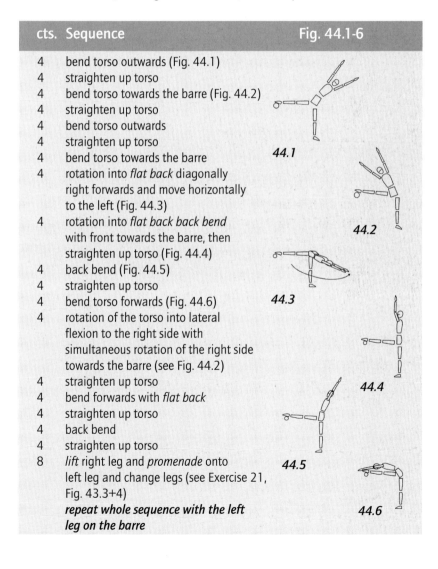
4	bend torso outwards (Fig. 44.1)	
4	straighten up torso	
4	bend torso towards the barre (Fig. 44.2)	
4	straighten up torso	
4	bend torso outwards	
4	straighten up torso	
4	bend torso towards the barre	*44.1*
4	rotation into *flat back* diagonally right forwards and move horizontally to the left (Fig. 44.3)	
4	rotation into *flat back back bend* with front towards the barre, then straighten up torso (Fig. 44.4)	*44.2*
4	back bend (Fig. 44.5)	
4	straighten up torso	
4	bend torso forwards (Fig. 44.6)	*44.3*
4	rotation of the torso into lateral flexion to the right side with simultaneous rotation of the right side towards the barre (see Fig. 44.2)	
4	straighten up torso	*44.4*
4	bend forwards with *flat back*	
4	straighten up torso	
4	back bend	
4	straighten up torso	
8	*lift* right leg and *promenade* onto left leg and change legs (see Exercise 21, Fig. 43.3+4)	*44.5*
	repeat whole sequence with the left leg on the barre	*44.6*

EXERCISE 23: "SIDE SPLIT"

Terms
passé	tip of the toe rotated outwards or brought parallel next to the knee
développé	development of the lower leg into stretched position

Effect
Apart from the extensive lengthening of the legs and the torso, the exercise also trains torso strength and holding power of the legs (thighs, knee extensors, outwards rotators).

Level of difficulty
Grade 2 ↑ (for grade 1 in simplified version, see Model Lesson 1)

Technical characteristics and execution
For the exact positions of the body in the lengthening exercises, see Exercises 21, 22. The slow development of the free leg through the outwardly rotated *passé* position to placing the straightened leg onto the barre and lifting and lowering it again requires concentric and excentric strength (cf. section 3.1.2). The torso must not move towards the other side.

Starting position: standing facing the barre in turned-out 1st position, both hands are on the barre.

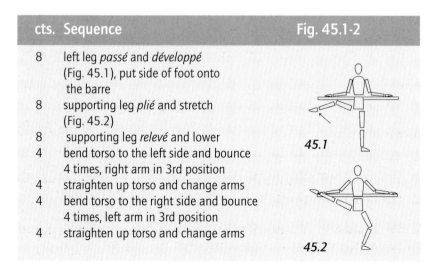

cts.	Sequence	Fig. 45.1-2
8	left leg *passé* and *développé* (Fig. 45.1), put side of foot onto the barre	
8	supporting leg *plié* and stretch (Fig. 45.2)	
8	supporting leg *relevé* and lower	
4	bend torso to the left side and bounce 4 times, right arm in 3rd position	
4	straighten up torso and change arms	
4	bend torso to the right side and bounce 4 times, left arm in 3rd position	
4	straighten up torso and change arms	

45.1

45.2

cts. Sequence (continued)	Fig. 45.3-4

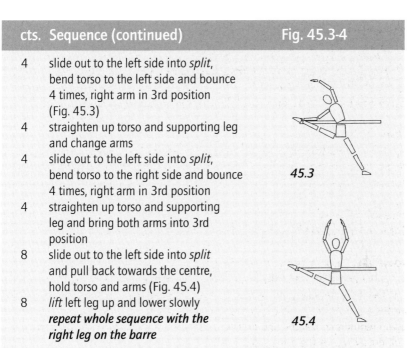

4   slide out to the left side into *split*,
    bend torso to the left side and bounce
    4 times, right arm in 3rd position
    (Fig. 45.3)
4   straighten up torso and supporting leg
    and change arms
4   slide out to the left side into *split*,
    bend torso to the right side and bounce
    4 times, right arm in 3rd position
4   straighten up torso and supporting
    leg and bring both arms into 3rd
    position
8   slide out to the left side into *split*
    and pull back towards the centre,
    hold torso and arms (Fig. 45.4)
8   *lift* left leg up and lower slowly
    **repeat whole sequence with the
    right leg on the barre**

45.3

45.4

EXERCISE 24: "SPLIT SIDE; BACK AND FORWARD"

Terms
relevé   pull up, *lift* into high ball stand or high toe stand

Effect
cf. Exercises 21, 22, 23.

Level of difficulty
Grade 3 ↑

Technical characteristics and execution
cf. other exercises at the barre.

Starting position: standing facing the barre, right leg rests on the barre, both legs
are turned out, hands hold on to the barre.

cts.	Sequence	Fig. 46.1-6

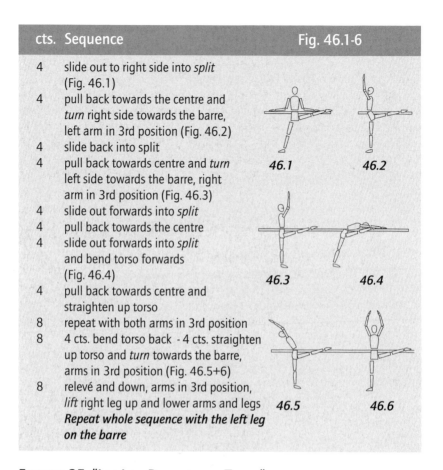

4	slide out to right side into *split* (Fig. 46.1)
4	pull back towards the centre and *turn* right side towards the barre, left arm in 3rd position (Fig. 46.2)
4	slide back into split
4	pull back towards centre and *turn* left side towards the barre, right arm in 3rd position (Fig. 46.3)
4	slide out forwards into *split*
4	pull back towards the centre
4	slide out forwards into *split* and bend torso forwards (Fig. 46.4)
4	pull back towards centre and straighten up torso
8	repeat with both arms in 3rd position
8	4 cts. bend torso back - 4 cts. straighten up torso and *turn* towards the barre, arms in 3rd position (Fig. 46.5+6)
8	relevé and down, arms in 3rd position, *lift* right leg up and lower arms and legs
	Repeat whole sequence with the left leg on the barre

46.1   46.2   46.3   46.4   46.5   46.6

EXERCISE 25: "LEG LIFT; BALANCE AND TURNS"

Terms

relevé	pull up, *lift* into high ball stand or high toe stand
cou-de-pied	foot of the free leg brought next to the ankle
développé	development of the lower leg into straightened position
préparation	preparation for *turns*

Effect

Development of the holding power of the free leg and of the ability to stand on one leg. This exercise aims at promoting the ability to balance the body vertically over a small supporting surface on one leg in *relevé* and at getting balance mechanisms used to rotations around the vertical axis of the body (*turns*).

Level of difficulty
Grade 3 ↑

Technical characteristics and execution
The barre serves as a means of maintaining balance and orientation in the preparation for *turns (préparation)* and in the *turns* themselves. The slow *lifting* of the straightened leg upwards to the front and the upwards bouncing at the highest possible point train the holding power of the front *quadriceps* and the *iliopsoas*. In this, the torso remains completely vertical (no back bend to lift the leg higher!), and the pelvis does not move backwards or to the sides because the abdominals, the buttocks and the abductors are tensed.

Lifting the body into the *relevé* position on one supporting leg, balancing the body vertically over the minimal support surface and holding this position all serve as preparation for the *turns* in *relevé*. Opening the leg fast to the side and closing the lower leg to the *passé* position in connection with the arm movement provides the impetus for rotation, leading to half a *turn*, and, with appropriate practice, to a full *turn* or more. The end of the *turn* is controlled by pulling the other shoulder backwards, by fixing the eyes in the new direction, and by opening the arms fast and holding on to the barre.

Starting position: right side towards the barre, standing in 5th *jazz position* (see section 3.3) turned out, right hand holds on to the barre, left arm in 2nd position.

cts.	Sequence	Fig. 47.1-2

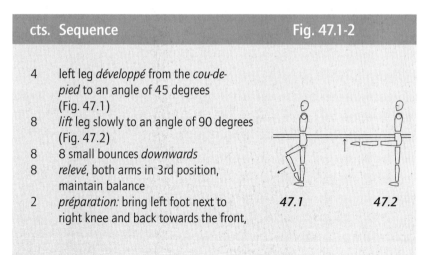

cts.	Sequence
4	left leg *développé* from the *cou-de-pied* to an angle of 45 degrees (Fig. 47.1)
8	*lift* leg slowly to an angle of 90 degrees (Fig. 47.2)
8	8 small bounces *downwards*
8	*relevé*, both arms in 3rd position, maintain balance
2	*préparation:* bring left foot next to right knee and back towards the front,

47.1   *47.2*

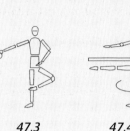

cts. Sequence (continued)   Fig. 47.3-4

left arm in 1st position (Fig. 47.3+4)
2   close left lower leg with *passé* on the
     right knee and 1 *turn en dehors*
· 4   repeat *préparation* and 1 *turn
     en dehors* (see above)
4   repeat *préparation* and 1 1/2 *turns
     en dehors* so that the left side is now
     turned towards the barre and put left
     foot down backwards
     *repeat whole sequence for the
     other side*

47.3   *47.4*

Exercise 26: "Contraction Fall and Jazz Split"

Terms
contraction fall   fall and roll down from a position of *contraction*

Effect
Development of the ability to combine dance sequences in which various
techniques are linked with each other across several spatial planes.

Level of difficulty
Grade 3 ↑ (individual techniques can be prepared separately from grade 2
onwards, cf. section 5)

Technical characteristics and execution
Falls are a further typical form of movement attributed to *Modern Dance*. Here,
dancers move as if they were falling from one position and one spatial plane into
another. *Falls* can be forwards, backwards, sideways, diagonally across and with
rotation (cf. **Centre Work 3**). Each form requires its own special technique for
catching the *fall* in a well-coordinated way, to absorb it and to extend it into a
new movement.

The *fall* practised in **part I** of the following exercise starts from a standing
position on both feet with a *contraction* onto the knees. It is interrupted just
before the knees touch the floor and transformed into a body roll sideways over
the thigh onto the stomach. This technique requires good *contraction*, strong

thigh and torso muscles and coordinated support work of the arms. Preparatory exercises on the floor are necessary (cf. *Floor Work*) before this *fall* can be executed precisely. The barre allows the trainees, if they have not yet developed enough strength, to catch themselves by holding on to it.

In *part II* of the sequence, lengthening in the *jazz split* position is added. In contrast to the normal *split*, the rear leg is bent in a large *attitude* position in the *jazz split*, with the knee not touching the floor. For fast rotations into this position from various starting positions or for controlled sliding out into the *jazz split* and pulling up out of the *jazz split*, the foremost requirement is strength of the buttocks and the back muscles. Exercises to promote this are integrated into the following sequence, but at beginner levels they can also be treated separately.

Starting position: right side towards the barre, parallel stand with feet spread at hip width, left arm in 3rd position, right hand holds onto the barre.

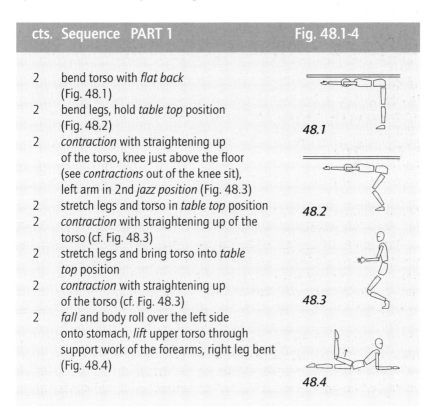

cts.	Sequence PART 1	Fig. 48.1-4

2	bend torso with *flat back* (Fig. 48.1)	
2	bend legs, hold *table top* position (Fig. 48.2)	**48.1**
2	*contraction* with straightening up of the torso, knee just above the floor (see *contractions* out of the knee sit), left arm in 2nd *jazz position* (Fig. 48.3)	
2	stretch legs and torso in *table top* position	**48.2**
2	*contraction* with straightening up of the torso (cf. Fig. 48.3)	
2	stretch legs and bring torso into *table top* position	
2	*contraction* with straightening up of the torso (cf. Fig. 48.3)	**48.3**
2	*fall* and body roll over the left side onto stomach, *lift* upper torso through support work of the forearms, right leg bent (Fig. 48.4)	
		48.4

cts. Sequence PART 2	Fig. 49.1-4

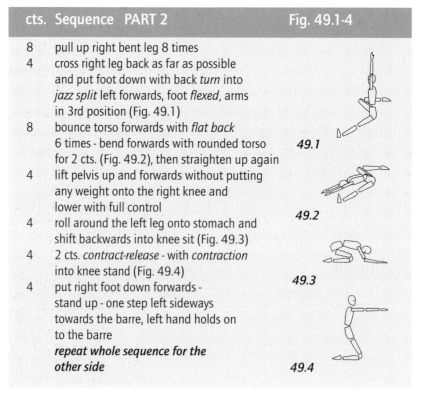

8	pull up right bent leg 8 times
4	cross right leg back as far as possible and put foot down with back *turn* into *jazz split* left forwards, foot *flexed*, arms in 3rd position (Fig. 49.1)
8	bounce torso forwards with *flat back* 6 times - bend forwards with rounded torso for 2 cts. (Fig. 49.2), then straighten up again
4	lift pelvis up and forwards without putting any weight onto the right knee and lower with full control
4	roll around the left leg onto stomach and shift backwards into knee sit (Fig. 49.3)
4	2 cts. *contract-release* - with *contraction* into knee stand (Fig. 49.4)
4	put right foot down forwards - stand up - one step left sideways towards the barre, left hand holds on to the barre **repeat whole sequence for the other side**

49.1

49.2

49.3

49.4

3.4.5 Floor Work 2

The main theme in the collection of exercises for **Floor Work 2** is the development of strength in the torso and leg muscles, and the preparation of dance positions and gestures such as *passé, attitude, développé, battement and rond de jambe.*

EXERCISE 27: "LEG WORK"

Terms

rond de jambe	large circular movement of the leg

Effect

Active mobility of the hip joints and strengthening of the stomach and leg muscles as well as the thigh *lifter*. Development of the *rond de jambes.*

Level of difficulty
Grade 3 ↑ (for grade 2 in simplified version, see Model Lesson 2)

Technical characteristics and execution
When lifting, lowering, abducting and circulating the straight legs while lying on the back, the pelvis must be fixed to the floor to avoid incorrect posture and incorrect strain on the lumbar vertebrae. For this reason, this exercise should only be done with advanced learners who have already built up enough strength in their abdominals to be able to fix the pelvis in upright position. At beginner levels, the exercise can be partly incorporated with support of the forearms and with the pelvis tilted backwards.

Starting position: lying straight on the back, arms in 2nd position.

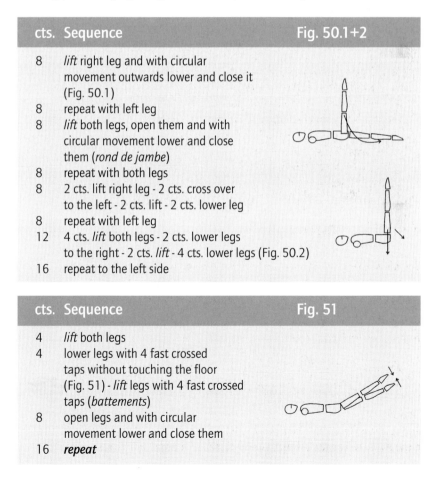

cts.	Sequence	Fig. 50.1+2
8	*lift* right leg and with circular movement outwards lower and close it (Fig. 50.1)	
8	repeat with left leg	
8	*lift* both legs, open them and with circular movement lower and close them (*rond de jambe*)	
8	repeat with both legs	
8	2 cts. lift right leg - 2 cts. cross over to the left - 2 cts. lift - 2 cts. lower leg	
8	repeat with left leg	
12	4 cts. *lift* both legs - 2 cts. lower legs to the right - 2 cts. *lift* - 4 cts. lower legs (Fig. 50.2)	
16	repeat to the left side	

cts.	Sequence	Fig. 51
4	*lift* both legs	
4	lower legs with 4 fast crossed taps without touching the floor (Fig. 51) - *lift* legs with 4 fast crossed taps (*battements*)	
8	open legs and with circular movement lower and close them	
16	*repeat*	

Exercise 28: "Leg Work Back"

Effect
Strengthening of the buttocks, and the rear leg and the back extensor muscles.

Level of difficulty
Grade 1 ↑

Technical characteristics and execution
While lying on the stomach, the legs are *lifted* backwards, held, bounced and lowered, with and without the support of the forearms. The bones of the pelvis remain in contact with the floor throughout, so that little strain is put on the lumbar vertebrae and the groin is actively lengthened.

Starting position: lying on the stomach, forehead rests on the hands.

cts.	Sequence	Fig. 52.1-4
4	3 cts. *lift* right leg - 1 ct. lower leg (Fig. 52.1)	
4	repeat with left leg	
4	repeat with both legs	*52.1*
4	repeat with both legs **lift upper body and support on forearms**	
4	3 cts. *lift* right leg - 1 ct. lower leg	
4	repeat with left leg	*52.2*
8	*lift* bent right leg 7 times - 1 ct. straighten and lower leg (Fig. 52.2)	
8	repeat with left leg	
8	*lift* legs, torso and arms and hold (Fig. 52.3)	*52.3*
4	lower	
4	to compensate, bring rounded back onto thighs in knee sit (Fig. 52.4)	
		52.4

Exercise 29: "Roll Up and Down"

Effect
The aim is to strengthen the abdominals and the *iliopsoas* with concentric and excentric muscle work.

Level of difficulty
Grade 3 ↑ (for grade 1+2 in simplified version, see Model Lesson 1+2)

Technical characteristics and execution
While lying on the back, first with the feet flat on the floor then with straightened legs, the torso is rolled up very slowly from the head forewards onto the thighs, then diagonally across to the right and to the left side of the legs. It is then rolled down again vertebra by vertebra. To make the exercise easier, the arms are extended to the front; to make it more difficult, the hands are clasped behind the neck. The shoulders remain pulled down and the chin, which is bent towards the chest, should not be "tucked in". Consistent breathing must be ensured.

Starting position: lying on the back, feet flat on the floor, arms next to the body.

cts.	Sequence	Fig. 53.1-4
16	8 cts. roll up, arms pull forwards - 8 cts. roll down (Fig. 53.1+2)	
16	8 cts. roll up towards the right side, arms pull next to right knee - 8 cts. roll down, repeat to the left side	*53.1*
16	*repeat sequence 2 times with 4 cts. for each stage, and then 4 times with 2 cts. for each stage* *repeat whole sequence, hands clasped behind the neck, elbows opened to the sides (Fig. 53.3)*	*53.2*
8	roll up with straight legs, arms forwards	
8	bounce rounded torso deeply 8 times, *flex* feet (Fig. 53.3)	*53.3*
8	roll down *repeat sequence twice with 4 cts. for each stage*	*53.4*

EXERCISE 30: "COCCYX BALANCES"

Terms

attitude   slightly bent leg position

Effect
This exercise trains the swift overcoming of gravity from lying on the back to a sitting position as well as the holding power of all muscles in extraordinary balance situations.

Level of difficulty
Grade 3 ↑

Technical characteristics and execution
Sitting up fast from lying straight on the back into the *coccyx balance* and balancing the body bent at the hip on the *coccyx* is an exercise from the HORTON technique. It is a special training exercise and requires good control of the whole body. In the *coccyx balance* position, the torso is straight and at an angle of approximately 45 degrees to the thighs, the lower legs are parallel to the floor or are stretched and bent alternately. This position is held for some time and slowly rolled down again rounded into a lying position, with torso and legs moving back towards the floor simultaneously. The following sequence of exercises starts with a preparatory stage in which the feet are still flat on the floor.

Starting position: lying on the back, feet are flat on the floor, arms in 2nd position (arms are in 1st position in the Figures).

cts.	Sequence	Fig. 54.1-3
4	sit up fast, feet remain flat on the floor, straighten torso and hold (Fig. 54.1)	
4	roll down rounded	
8	repeat	
4	sit up fast into *coccyx balance* and hold (Fig. 54.2)	
4	roll down torso and legs simultaneously	
4	sit up fast into *coccyx balance* and hold	
2	*turn* onto right hip, legs remain bent (Fig. 54.3)	
	twist upper body to the right and support backwards with bent arms, left leg backwards in *attitude* position	
2	sit up into *coccyx balance*	
4	roll down torso and legs simultaneously	

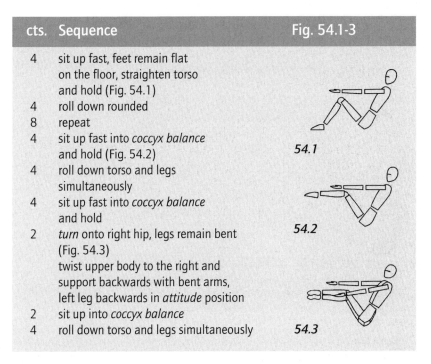

54.1

54.2

54.3

Starting position: lying straight on the back (HORTON).

cts.	Sequence	Fig. 55.1+2
8	sit up fast into *coccyx balance* and hold	
4	roll down	
8	sit up fast into *coccyx balance* and hold	
8	stretch right leg and hold (Fig. 55.1)	
8	stretch left leg and hold	
8	bend right leg and hold	
8	bend left leg and hold	
8	stretch both legs and hold (Fig. 55.2)	
8	bend both legs and hold	
4	roll down	
	repeat last sequence with 4 cts. resp. 2 cts. for each stage	

EXERCISE 31: "COCCYX BALANCE AND STRETCHES"

Terms
flex-point   bending and stretching the foot

Effect
See Exercise 29 with reinforced lengthening of the leg.

Level of difficulty
Grade 3 ↑

Technical characteristics and execution
The back remains straight in spite of extreme lengthening and balancing position.

Starting position: sitting level with legs bent, tips of the toes touch the floor, hands around thighs.

cts.	Sequence	Fig. 56.1+2

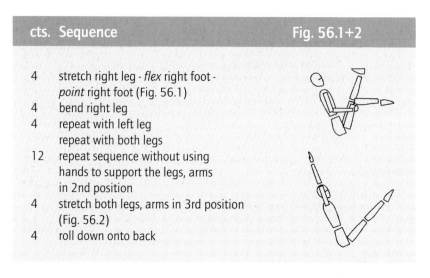

cts.	Sequence
4	stretch right leg - *flex* right foot - *point* right foot (Fig. 56.1)
4	bend right leg
4	repeat with left leg
	repeat with both legs
12	repeat sequence without using hands to support the legs, arms in 2nd position
4	stretch both legs, arms in 3rd position (Fig. 56.2)
4	roll down onto back

EXERCISE 32: "LEG STRETCHING"

Terms
flex-point   bending and stretching the foot

Effect
Passive lengthening of the hip extensors and the rear leg muscles.

Level of difficulty
Grade 3 ↑

Technical characteristics and execution
While lying on the back, the free leg, lifted 90 degrees vertically, is lengthened by pulling with the arms and flexing the foot. The lying leg (supporting leg), the back and the pelvis remain straight on the floor, the shoulder girdle is consciously pulled downwards.

Starting position: lying on the back, arms in 2nd position.

cts.	Sequence	Fig. 57.1-3
4	bend right knee and straighten up vertically (Fig. 57.1)	
8	4 times foot *flex-point*, flex again on ct. 8	
4	slow *plié*, sole of the foot parallel to the ceiling (Fig. 57.2)	*57.1*
4	straighten leg with *flexed* foot	
8	*plié* and repeat straightening	
8	*plié* and repeat straightening while pulling the thigh towards the chest with both hands	*57.2*
8	repeat	
8	pull straight leg towards chest 8 times, foot *pointed* (Fig. 57.3)	
4	lower leg	
	repeat sequence with left leg	*57.3*

Exercise 33: "Battements"

Terms

battements	thrusts of the leg
flex-point	bending and stretching the foot
développé	development of the lower leg into stretched position
passé	tip of the toe rotated outwards or brought parallel next to the knee

Effect
Mobility in the hip joint and active lengthening of the legs in all planes of movement.

Level of difficulty
Grade 2 ↑ (for grade 1 in simplified version, see Model Lesson 1)

Technical characteristics and execution
Battements are fast straight thrusts of the legs while lying on the back, on the side or on the stomach. Especially in the unstable side position, the torso must be fixed by tensing the abdominals and the buttocks. Backwards or forwards motion of the pelvis must be avoided. These fast thrusts are prepared with slow developments of the legs and *flex-points*.

Starting position: lying on the back with forearms supporting.

cts.	Sequence	Fig. 58.1-4

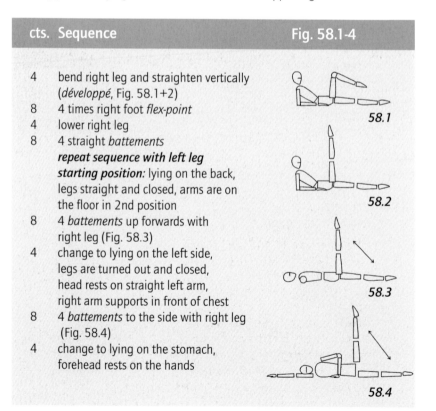

4	bend right leg and straighten vertically (*développé*, Fig. 58.1+2)	
8	4 times right foot *flex-point*	
4	lower right leg	58.1
8	4 straight *battements*	
	repeat sequence with left leg	
	starting position: lying on the back,	
	legs straight and closed, arms are on	
	the floor in 2nd position	58.2
8	4 *battements* up forwards with	
	right leg (Fig. 58.3)	
4	change to lying on the left side,	
	legs are turned out and closed,	
	head rests on straight left arm,	
	right arm supports in front of chest	58.3
8	4 *battements* to the side with right leg	
	(Fig. 58.4)	
4	change to lying on the stomach,	
	forehead rests on the hands	

58.4

cts.	Sequence (continued)	Fig. 58.5

8	4 *battements* backwards with right leg (Fig. 58.5)	
4	change to lying on the right side, legs are turned out and closed, head rests on straight right arm, left arm supports in front of chest	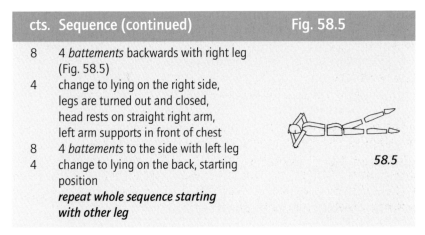
8	4 *battements* to the side with left leg	
4	change to lying on the back, starting position **repeat whole sequence starting with other leg**	*58.5*

Starting position: lying on the right side, legs turned out, head rests on straight right arm, left arm supports in front of body.

cts.	Sequence	Fig. 59.1-4

2	left leg *passé* and straightened vertically (Fig. 59.1)	
2	lower leg with *flexed foot*	
4	repeat	
16	8 straight *battements* (Fig. 59.2)	*59.1*
2	4 fast, small parallel *battements* with *flexed foot* (Fig. 59.3)	
1	1 *battement* parallel up to the limit of the hip joint, turn out fast and thrust up as far as possible with *point*	*59.2*
1	lower leg with rotation into parallel position with *flexed foot*	
4	4 fast and high *battements* with rotation, repeat	*59.3*
8	*lift* legs and upper body and balance arms in 3rd position (Fig. 59.4)	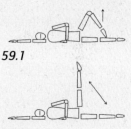
4	body roll over the back onto the left side and repeat whole sequence with right leg	 *59.4*

Exercise 34: "Hip Stretching"

Terms

hip stretching	lengthening of the groin
swastika	sitting with one leg bent in at the front and the other bent in at the back (4th position)

Effect
Lengthening of the hip flexors and the leg *lifters*.

Level of difficulty
Grade 3 ↑

Technical characteristics and execution
Starting in the 4th position, then while lying on the back, the hip of the leg bent in at the back is actively raised forwards and lowered again. This lengthening is then reinforced by straightening the leg at the front with *flex-point* and by pulling the rear lower leg towards the body.

Starting position: *swastika* sit (4th position), right leg to the front, left leg bent in at the back, forearms support at the back.

cts.	Sequence	Fig. 60
4	stretch left hip forwards and upwards (Fig. 60)	
4	lower left hip back onto floor	
8	repeat and slide out fast into lying on the back, legs remain in 4th position, arms in 2nd position	
4	stretch left hip forwards and upwards	
4	lower left hip back onto floor	
8	repeat, then pull left lower leg towards body with left arm and straighten right leg, *flex foot*	
4	with right foot in *point* position, stretch left hip forwards and upwards	
4	with *flex* of right foot lower left hip onto floor	
8	repeat	
	repeat whole sequence starting with other leg	

3.4.6 Centre Work 3

In the section *Centre Work 3* of the catalogue of exercises according to ALAIN BERNARD, descriptions are given of a few preparatory exercises first and then further *special techniques* like *lay outs* and *falls* which can be performed in *Jazz Dance at advanced levels* (from grade *3 onwards*). The level of difficulty and the effect of the individual techniques will therefore not be explicitly described in all exercises.

EXERCISE 35: "FEET CIRCLE AND BALANCE"

Terms

relevé	pull up, *lift* into high ball stand or high toe stand
plié	bending the legs

Effect
Stability on one leg in connection with isolated movements of the free leg.

Technical characteristics and execution
Isolated movement of the foot of the free leg in coordination with forwards, sideways and backwards movement as well as bending and straightening of the free leg. The foot is circled inwards and outwards during the leg gesture. Balance must be maintained on the supporting leg. Both legs remain rotated outwards, the free knee as far as possible at the starting point.

The exercise is made more difficult through a bend-stretch-coordination in which a slow *plié* is performed in the supporting leg during the straightening phase and a stretch during the bending phase of the free leg. With advanced dancers, this whole sequence can be done directly with the *flex-point* combination (cf. p.62).

Starting position: standing on left leg with outward rotation, right foot placed on front of left ankle, arms in 2nd position (Fig. 61.1).

cts. Sequence

Fig. 61.1-4

PART 1

4 stretch right leg forwards with
4 circles of the foot outwards
(Fig. 61.2)

4 bend right leg and bring it next to
body with 4 circles of the foot inwards

4 stretch right leg to the side with
4 circles of the foot outwards
(Fig. 61.3)

61.1

4 bend right leg and bring it next to
body with 4 circles of the foot inwards,
place foot against back of left leg

4 stretch right leg backwards with 4 circles
of the foot outwards (Fig. 61.4)

4 bend right leg and and bring it next
to body with 4 circles of the foot inwards,
place foot against back of left leg

4 stretch right leg to the side with 4 circles
of the foot outwards

61.2

4 bend right leg and bring it next to
body with 4 circles of the foot inwards,
set right foot backwards onto floor and
place left foot in front of right ankle
*repeat sequence with left leg and
alternate legs*

PART 2

4 stretch right leg forwards with
4 circles of the foot outwards,
simultaneously *plié* in the supporting leg

61.3

4 bend right leg and bring next to left leg
with 4 circles of the foot inwards, stretch
supporting leg simultaneously
*repeat sequence side, back, side and then
with left leg (cf. PART 1)*

PART 3

*repeat sequence at double speed
with 2 cts. for each stage*

614

EXERCISE 36: "BRUSHES AND BATTEMENTS"

Terms
battements   45 degrees and 90 degrees thrusts with straightened leg

Effect
Training precise, vigorous legwork in standing.

Level of difficulty
Grade 3 ↑ (for grade 1+2 in simplified version, see Model Lesson 1+2)

Technical characteristics and execution
When doing *brushes*, the foot of the free leg sweeps full-sole including the tips of the toes forwards and to the sides (also backwards, not included here) and is brought back to the supporting leg along the same path. This gesture is extended to a *battement* at angles of 45 and 90 degrees. The *brushes* and *battements* are practised in *Jazz Dance* in parallel position and with outwards rotation, with the parallel *battement* to the sides only achieving a modest height because of the limits of the hip joint. The pelvis remains fixed in the neutral position throughout.

Starting position: 1st position parallel, arms in neutral position.

cts.	Sequence	Fig. 62.1-2
8	8 *brushes* to the right side forwards, the emphasis is on sweeping the foot out (Fig. 62.1)	
8	8 *brushes* to the left side forwards	
8	8 *battements* to the right side to 45 degrees (Fig. 62.2)	
8	8 *battements* to the left side to 45 degrees	

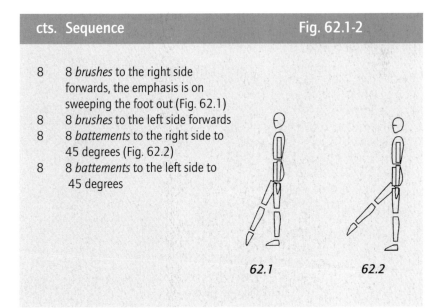

62.1   62.2

cts.	Sequence (continued)	Fig. 62.3
8	8 *battements* to the right side to 90 degrees (Fig. 62.3)	
8	8 *battements* to the left side to 90 degrees	
8	8 *brushes* to the right side	
8	8 *brushes* to the left side	
4	4 *brushes* to the right side	
4	4 *brushes* to the left side	
2	2 *brushes* to the right side	
2	2 *brushes* to the left side	
8	8 *brushes* alternating between the right side and the left side	

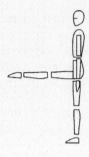

62.3

cts.	Sequence (continued)	Fig. 63
4	*plié - turn legs out in 1st position - stretch legs - sweep right foot to the side* (Fig. 63)	
8	8 *brushes* to the right side, the emphasis is now on bringing the foot back to the other leg	
8	8 *brushes* to the left side	
4	4 *brushes* to the right side	
4	4 *brushes* to the left side	
4	4 *brushes* to the right side	
2	2 *brushes* to the left side	
8	8 *brushes* changing between the right side and the left side	
4	finish sequence with a *plié*	

EXERCISE 37: "RELEASE SWINGS AND LAY OUT SIDE"

Terms

release swing	*released swing* of the torso from one side to the other
lay out side	bending the straight torso to the sides, with the free leg raised in the opposite direction

Effect
All *lay out* forms described below place substantial demands on general flexibility and balance, and on the ability to regain equilibrium in unstable positions.

Technical characteristics and execution
In the *release swing*, an exercise from the HORTON-technique, starting in the *flat back* position and via a *release* position, the torso is swung from one side to the other. In *contrast to the horizontal swings* in which the torso remains parallel to the floor (cf. **Centre Work 2**), here the whole back including the head is relaxed as it passes in front of the legs and is then brought back into the *flat back* position at the other end of the swing. *Release swings* require constant alternation between tension and relaxation of all torso muscles. They are further developed into circle swings and into a *lay out* position to the sides, also called *T-Position* in the HORTON-technique. In the *lay out side* position described below, it is essential to ensure good alignment of the front of the body forwards and to avoid backwards movement of the pelvis.

A *lay out* is always a balance position on one supporting leg in which the whole torso, in one line with the free leg, is tilted forwards, sideways or backwards. The *lay out* back is less extended due to the mobility limits of the hip joint and the spine when bending backwards.

Starting position: large 2nd position, torso forwards with *flat back*, arms in 3rd position.

cts.	Sequence	Fig. 64.1-2
16	8 *release swings*, starting towards the left side (Fig. 64.1, 8 times)	
4	*release swings* to the left and to the right side	
4	*release swings* to the left side, straighten up and turn torso upwards then to the right side (Fig. 64.2) into the *flat back* position and *release swing* to the left side	
8	repeat sequence for the other side	
4	*release swings* to the left and to the right side	

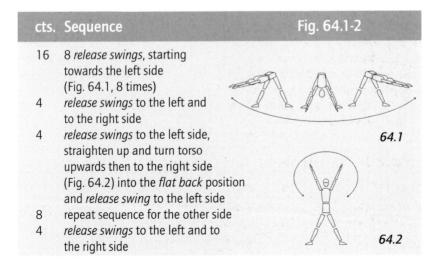

64.1

64.2

cts. Sequence (continued)	Fig. 64.3

2   *release swings* to the left side with
    1 circle upwards and *lay out* to the
    right side (Fig. 64.3)
4   hold balance position over the
    right leg
2   straighten up torso into 2nd position,
    arms in 3rd position
12   repeat sequence for the other side

643

EXERCISE 38: "LAY OUT FORWARD"

Terms

lay out forward	tilting the straightened torso forwards, free leg extended to one side
passé	point of the foot turned out or parallel next to the knee
flat back	bending the torso backwards while the back is stretched
arabesque	extending straight free leg backwards

Technical characteristics and execution

After moving the outwardly rotated free leg upwards to one side, the straight torso bends forwards with an extended pull, the head remains in line with the spine. The leg fixed sideways (no movement back into the *arabesque* position!) is rolled in by the tilting of the pelvis and produces a counter pull outwards.

Starting position: standing, feet in 1st position parallel, arms in 2nd *jazz position*.

cts. Sequence 1	Fig. 65. 1+2

4	right leg in *passé* parallel position - stretch leg out forwards and move to the side with bent foot (Fig. 65.1)
4	bend torso forwards with *flat back*, the right leg, extended to the side, is turned forwards by tilting the pelvis (Fig. 65.2)
4	take 1 ct. to straighten up torso - take 1 ct. to perform outwardly rotated *passé* to the right side - take 1 ct. to go into *passé* parallel position to the right side - take 1 ct. to lower leg to the right side
12	repeat with left leg

Technical characteristics and execution
The free leg is moved over the side back into the *arabesque* position and forms a single line with the torso which is tilted forwards as far as possible, with head extended and foot *flexed*.

cts. Sequence 2	Fig. 66

4	right leg in *passé* parallel position - stretch leg out forwards with *flexed* foot and move it backwards turned out over the side
4	*lay out* forward, torso and leg form a single line (Fig. 66)
4	take 2 cts. to straighten up torso and move into *passé* parallel position - take 2 cts. to lower right leg
12	repeat with left leg

Technical characteristics and execution
In this variation of *the lay out forwards*, the free leg is moved directly backwards out of the *passé* parallel position and the torso is simultaneously bent forwards with an extended pull.

cts. Sequence 3	see Fig. 66
4	right leg in *passé* parallel position - stretch backwards and torso *lay out forwards* (cf. Fig. 66)
4	take 1 ct. to turn right leg out, foot *flexed* - take 3 cts. to straighten up torso and simultaneously extend outwardly rotated right leg to the side
4	right leg in outwardly rotated *passé* position - move into *passé* parallel position and lower leg

EXERCISE 39: "LAY OUT BACK"

Technical characteristics and execution
After developing the free leg forwards out of the 90 degrees *passé* position, the torso bends backwards with *lift* and with *flat back*.

Starting position: standing, feet in 1st position parallel, arms in 2nd *jazz position*.

cts. Sequence	Fig. 67
4 right leg in *passé* parallel position and bend forwards, foot *flexed*	
4 torso *flat back back bend* (Fig. 67)	
4 take 2 cts. to straighten up torso - take 1 ct. to go into *passé* parallel position with right leg - take 1 ct. to lower right leg	
12 repeat with left leg	

EXERCISE 40: "CONTRACTION PLIÉS AND TWIST"

Terms

contraction pliés	deep *plié* with *contraction* of the pelvis
twist	twisting the torso counter to the pelvis

Technical characteristics and execution

This exercise serves as preparation for *falls* in all directions. The *contractions* have already been practised at the barre and are described in the section *"Barre"*. Here they are executed starting in an upright stand, with the legs moving into a *plié-relevé* position through the *contraction* in the centre. A further new feature is the *twisting* of torso and arms counter to the *contraction* of the pelvis, a movement applied in the *back fall*.

Starting position: 2nd position parallel, arms in 2nd position

cts.	Sequence	Fig. 68.1+2
4	deepen the *contraction* and the *plié*; arms are moved out of the centre into 1st position. (Fig. 6.8.1)	
4	straighten up and stretch - lower the heels	
8	repeat	
4	*contraction*, deepen the *plié* and *twist* torso simultaneously to the right side (Fig. 68.2), open arms to the front and to the back downwards parallel to the twisted shoulder girdle	
4	straighten up and stretch - lower heels	
8	repeat	
	repeat whole sequence with 2 cts. and then 1 ct. for each stage	

EXERCISE 41: "BACK FALL"

Terms

twist	*twisting* the torso counter to the pelvis
contraction plié	deepened *plié* with *contraction* of the pelvis

Technical characteristics and execution

As described in section 3.4.4., Exercise 26, *falls* are another typical form of movement attributed to *Modern Dance* and *Jazz Dance*. Here, dancers move as if they were falling from one position and one spatial plane into another. *Falls* can be forwards, backwards, sideways, diagonally across and with rotation. Each form requires its own special technique for catching the *fall* in a well-coordinated way, to absorb it and to extend it into a new movement.

In the *back fall*, the technique already described in Exercise 40 is applied. The *contraction plié* is deepened even further until the knees almost touch the floor. Then the torso is *twisted* counter to the pelvis and lowered backwards. When the rear shoulder touches the floor, the body slides out into lying straight on the back. Stand up via the one-sided sit with the left leg bent in, place the right foot flat onto the floor, straighten up and open the left foot sideways into 2nd position parallel. This *fall* technique derives from GRAHAM.

Starting position: 2nd position parallel, right arm in 3rd position, left hand touches left groin.

cts.	Sequence	Fig. 69
4	*contraction plié* (see Fig.68.1) and deepen	
4	*twist* backwards to the right, *fall* onto the right shoulder and slide out into lying on the back (Fig. 69)	
4	stand up over one-sided sit	
12	repeat with *twist* to the left side and *fall* onto right shoulder	

EXERCISE 42: FRONTFALL 1 "SPLIT FALL"

Technical characteristics and execution

This *fall* was taken from the GRAHAM-technique. From the 1st position parallel, the outwardly rotated right leg slides out into a large 2nd position, the main weight remains over the left leg, the left arm makes an inside circle simultaneously. With the arms forward in support, the left hip is turned towards the floor and the straightened torso is lowered towards the right leg without touching the floor. Standing up: cross left leg backwards and with *turn* backwards to the left side straighten up into a one-sided sit, bend in right leg, place left foot forwards onto floor, straighten up into stand and close feet (see also *CONTRACTION* FALL at the barre).

Starting position: 1st position parallel, arms in neutral position.

cts.	Sequence	Fig. 70.1+2
8	slide out slowly to the right and *front fall* (Fig. 70.1+2)	
4	stand up over one-sided sit with turn backwards	
12	*repeat sequence to the left*	

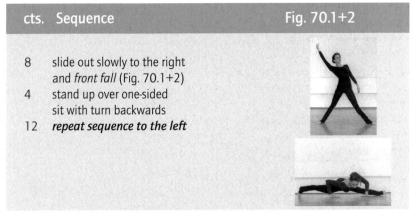

Exercise 43: Front fall 2 "Arabesque Fall"

Terms

arabesque	extending straight free leg backwards
turn dehors	outside turn, away from the supporting leg

Technical characteristics and execution

This *fall*, also a GRAHAM-technique, starts with a *lay out* of the torso from the 5th *jazz position* via the right leg, with the left leg extended in the *arabesque* position in line with the torso. Both hands are forward for support – the right foot slides out backwards until the sternum touches the floor. Standing up: cross left leg backwards and straighten up into knee stand with *turn* to the left side – place left foot onto floor forwards – move into stand, right arm forwards, and with 1 1/2 *turns* to the right move into the 5th *jazz position*, left foot forwards.

Starting position: 5th *jazz position* right foot forwards, arms in neutral position.

cts.	Sequence	Fig. 71
4	*lay out* forwards and slide out into *fall* (Fig. 71)	
4	turn over knee stand, straighten up into stand and 1 1/2 *turns dehors* to the right side	
8	repeat sequence to the left	

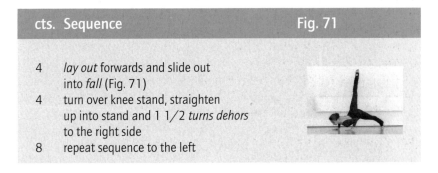

EXERCISE 44: FRONT FALL 3 "TWIST FALL"

Technical characteristics and execution

This *fall* is a combination of *contraction plié* and *front fall 1: "Split Fall"*. It starts in the 2nd position parallel with a *contraction plié* (cf. Fig. 68.1) which is deepened. Just before the knees touch the floor, body and legs are straightened and the torso is *twisted* to one side. One leg slides out with simultaneous arm circle (Fig. 72.1), and the torso is lowered with arms supporting into *front fall 1* (Fig. 72.2)

Fig. 72.1   *Fig. 72.2*

EXERCISE 45: "FRONT FALL 4"

Technical characteristics and execution

Sink to the knees with a *contraction plié* (Fig. 73.1) – straightened torso falls forwards, left arm supports forwards, right arm slides out forwards. The end position is lying on the stomach (Fig. 73.2). Stand up in the same way as in *front fall 1*. *Front fall 4* is a HORTON-technique.

Fig. 73.1   *Fig. 73.2*

EXERCISE 46: "SIDE FALL"

Technical characteristics and execution

In this example, a jump is transformed into a *side fall* from the HORTON-technique, a combined movement typical of *Modern Dance*. A *hop* (a jump in which starting leg and landing leg are identical) on the left foot is followed by a *passé* to the right side (Fig. 74.1). Landing in squat position, the instep of the free leg (not the knee!) touches the floor. The body rolls over the right hip and slides out into lying on the right side with brief support of the right and left arm (Fig. 74.2). Both legs are straight and closed, the right arm is under the head and in a single line with the body.

Fig. 74.1   *Fig. 74.2*

Fig. 75: Isolated side shift of the head   *Fig. 76: Isolated shoulder and chest/polycentrics*

3.4.7 Isolation

Effect and technique are described generally in section 3.2.

EXERCISE 47: "HEAD ISOLATION"

cts.	Starting position: 2nd position parallel, arms in neutral position
8	*turn* head twice to the right side - neutral position - *turn* head to the left side - neutral position
8	lower head twice - neutral position - *lift* head - neutral position
8	bend head twice to the right side - neutral position - bend head to the left side - neutral position
8	nod head twice towards the right side - neutral position - nod head to the left side - neutral position
8	2 head circles to the right side - backwards - to the left side - forwards
8	2 head circles to the left side

cts.	Starting position: press hands together tightly over head, fix shoulders
8	shift head 8 times to the right and to the left side (as in Fig. 75)
8	shift head 8 times forwards and backwards
8	shift head 8 times diagonally forwards to the right side and diagonally backwards to the left side
8	repeat 8 times for the other side
8	4 head circles in the horizontal plane to the right side
8	repeat 4 head circles to the left side

EXERCISE 48: "SHOULDER ISOLATION"

cts.	Starting position: 2nd position parallel, arms in 2nd jazz position
4	*lift* and lower right shoulder 4 times
4	*lift* and lower left shoulder 4 times
4	*lift* and lower both shoulders 4 times
8	*lift* and lower right and left shoulder alternately 8 times
8	shift right shoulder 4 times up and then forwards - backwards in half circle
8	repeat 4 times with left shoulder

cts.	
8	shift both shoulders 4 times up and then forwards - backwards in half circle
8	shift right and left shoulder alternately 8 times forwards - backwards
8	4 shoulder circles to the right side backwards
8	4 shoulder circles to the left side backwards
8	circle both shoulders backwards 4 times
8	4 shoulder circles to the right side forwards
8	4 shoulder circles to the left side forwards
8	circle both shoulders forwards 4 times

EXERCISE 49: "CHEST ISOLATION"

Starting position: 2nd position parallel, hands touch the groin.

cts.	Fig. 77: Isolation of head, chest, pelvis/polycentrics
8	shift chest 4 times to the right and to the left side
8	shift chest 4 times forwards - backwards
8	shift chest 4 times diagonally forwards to the right side - diagonally backwards to the left side
8	repeat 4 times for the other side
16	circle chest 4 times over the right side
16	circle chest 4 times over the left side

EXERCISE 50: "PELVIS ISOLATION"

Starting position: 2nd position parallel, arms in neutral position.

cts.	Fig. 78 Isolation of pelvis
8	bounce pelvis 4 times to the right side and 4 times to the left side
8	4 times *contract* - 4 times *release* (Fig. 78)
8	shift pelvis 4 times alternately to the right side diagonally forwards and to the left side diagonally backwards
8	shift pelvis 4 times alternately to the left side diagonally forwards and to the right side diagonally backwards
16	4 pelvis circles over the right side
16	4 pelvis circles over the left side

EXERCISE 51: "HAND ISOLATION"

Starting position: 2nd position parallel, arms extended forwards.

cts.	
8	8 hand circles outwards to the right side
8	8 hand circles outwards to the left side
8	8 hand circles inwards to the right side
8	8 hand circles inwards to the left side
8	spread right and left hand 8 times alternately and make fist
8	spread both hands 8 times and make fist

3.4.8 Across the Floor

Jazz walks, jazz turns and jumps are practised across the centre of the room or along the diagonal as the longest distance. In this section, a few forms are presented from the complete range.

JAZZ WALKS

Level of difficulty
Grade 2 ↑ (for grade 1 in simplified version, see Model Lesson 1)

Jazz walks are ways of moving while walking in which the rules of *polycentrics* are applied. Each step is connected with isolated movement of one or more parts of the body. *Jazz walks* can progress forwards, backwards, diagonally across or sideways through the room, and can be linked with *turns, jumps, falls, slides* and other ways of moving. There are no limits to the number of variations which constantly evolve in different forms out of the so-called *"jazz feeling"*, that intuitive feeling of the particular teacher and choreographer for music and rhythm.

For this reason, only a few basic forms are described here as appropriate for training at beginner levels. Advanced forms evolve in choreographies, depending on the music and on the theme.

EXERCISE 52: "STEP-TIP"

cts.	Sequence
1	step forwards on right foot, with ball on the floor, leg straightened
1	*tip* of left foot is put down next to ball of right foot without putting any weight over left foot: *tip*
1	step forwards on left foot, with ball on the floor, leg straightened
1	*tip* of right foot is put down next to ball of left foot without putting any weight over right foot: *tip*
	repeat continuously

Variation 1

2	step on right foot - *tip* on left foot (cf. above)
2	step on left foot - *tip* on right foot
4	step forwards on right foot - backwards on left foot - backwards on right foot - forwards on left foot. *Turn* hip slightly with each step. Repeat continuously, then start with the left foot.

Variation 2

2	step on right foot - *tip* on left foot (cf. above)
2	step on left foot - *tip* on right foot
4	1st ct.: step forwards on right foot - 2nd ct.: step backwards on left foot - 3rd ct.: pause - 4th ct. "and 4": step backwards on right foot, put weight briefly over the ball - step forwards on left foot (*ball change*) repeat continuously, then start with the left foot

EXERCISE 53: "CAT STEP"

cts.	Fig. 79

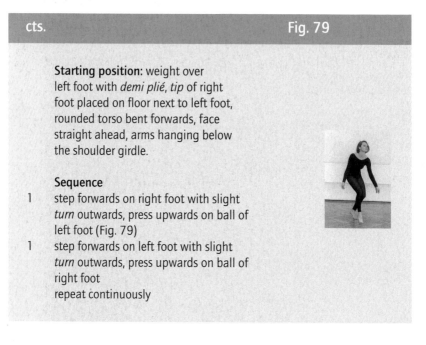

Starting position: weight over left foot with *demi plié*, *tip* of right foot placed on floor next to left foot, rounded torso bent forwards, face straight ahead, arms hanging below the shoulder girdle.

Sequence

1	step forwards on right foot with slight *turn* outwards, press upwards on ball of left foot (Fig. 79)
1	step forwards on left foot with slight *turn* outwards, press upwards on ball of right foot
	repeat continuously

Exercise 54: "Contraction Walk"

cts.	Fig. 80.1+2

Starting position: weight over left foot with *demi plié*, no weight over ball of right foot, ball is next to left foot.

Sequence

1   step forwards on right foot through *contraction*, put whole weight over right foot, left foot rests on ball (Fig. 80.1)
1   *release* (Fig. 80.2)
1   step forwards on left foot through *contraction*, put whole weight over left foot, left foot rests on ball (Fig. 80.1)
1   *release* (Fig. 80.1+2)
    repeat continuously

Variation

1   step forwards on right foot with *contraction - release*
1   put weight over right foot with *contraction - release*
1   put weight over left foot with *contraction - release*
1   put weight over right foot with *contraction - release*

EXERCISE 55: "SIDE WALK WITH LEG ROTATION"

cts.	Fig. 81

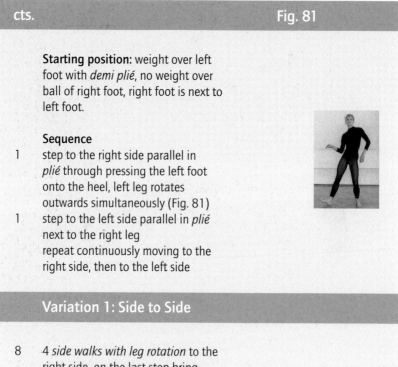

Starting position: weight over left foot with *demi plié*, no weight over ball of right foot, right foot is next to left foot.

Sequence

1   step to the right side parallel in *plié* through pressing the left foot onto the heel, left leg rotates outwards simultaneously (Fig. 81)

1   step to the left side parallel in *plié* next to the right leg repeat continuously moving to the right side, then to the left side

Variation 1: Side to Side

8   4 *side walks with leg rotation* to the right side, on the last step bring the left foot onto the ball (no weight over the ball) next to the right foot

8   4 *side walks with leg rotation* reversed

4   repeat 2 *side walks* to the right side

4   repeat 2 *side walks* to the left side

4   *side walks* to the right side and to the left side in direct alternation

Variation 2: Arm+Head Coordination

Starting position: arms in 1st *jazz position*, finger tips touch the sternum.

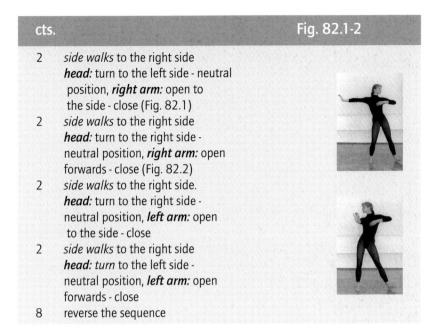

cts.	Fig. 82.1-2
2	*side walks* to the right side **head:** turn to the left side - neutral position, **right arm:** open to the side - close (Fig. 82.1)
2	*side walks* to the right side **head:** turn to the right side - neutral position, **right arm:** open forwards - close (Fig. 82.2)
2	*side walks* to the right side. **head:** turn to the right side - neutral position, **left arm:** open to the side - close
2	*side walks* to the right side **head:** *turn* to the left side - neutral position, **left arm:** open forwards - close
8	reverse the sequence

EXERCISE 56: "SIDE WALK WITH HIP SHIFT"

cts.	Sequence	Fig. 83
1	step to the right side parallel in *plié* by pressing upwards on the ball of the left foot while at the same time shifting the pelvis to the left side (Fig. 83, in the picture with simultaneous isolation of head and chest *polycentrics*)	
1	bring left foot next to right foot with weight over ball while at the same time shifting the pelvis to the right side repeat continuously, subsequently reversed with change of direction over 4 and 2 steps	

cts. Variation: Contract -Release

2   *side walks* to the right side with
     hip shift to the left side - right,
     simultaneously 2 times *contract -
     release*
     repeat continuously or change
     from *side to side*

EXERCISE 57: "JAZZ WALK AND TURN"

cts Sequence   Fig. 84.1+2

2   2 steps to the right side - step
     forwards on left foot with small *plié*,
     foot rolls down from the ball, arms
     move in opposite direction

1   step forwards on the right foot with
     plié, stretch left arm forwards for
     préparation, right arm is extended
     to the side (Fig. 84.1)

1   *turn* on left foot *en dehors* in *plié*,
     hook right foot into knee joint of
     left leg (Fig. 84.2)

4   repeat reversed, then continuously

COMBINATIONS

Level of difficulty
Grade 2 ↑

All *jazz walks* can be combined with each other in manifold ways and with other techniques such as *turns, jumps and falls.* Thus the techniques of the individual steps are practised, memorization of the individual movements trained and a certain repertoire of movements elaborated in preparation for dance choreography.

Three examples are given below of simple step combinations which can be practised at beginner levels.

Exercise 58: "Step-Tip + Side Walk-Leg Rotation"

cts.	Sequence
4	2 times *step-tip* forwards, starting on the right foot
4	2 *side walks* to the right: open - close - open - close with a *tip* without putting any weight over the foot
8	repeat, starting on the left foot
	repeat continuously, alternating between right foot and left foot

Exercise 59: "Contraction Walk + Side Walk-Hip Lift"

cts.	Sequence
4	*contraction walk* forwards on the right foot and on the left foot
4	4 *contraction walks* (at double speed)
8	4 *side walks* with *hip lift* to the right side, on last step bring foot next to leg without putting any weight over it
16	repeat, starting on the left foot
	repeat continuously, alternating between right foot and left foot

EXERCISE 60: "STEP-TIP-BALL CHANGE + SIDE WALK-ARM-HEAD-COORDINATION"

cts. Sequence

4	two times *step-tip* forwards, starting on right leg
4	1st ct.: one step forwards on the right foot - 2nd ct.: one step backwards on the left foot - 3rd ct.: pause - 4th ct. (and 4): step backwards on the right foot putting weight briefly on ball and one step forwards on the left foot (see Exercise 52, variation 2)
8	arm + head coordination to the right side (see Exercise 55, variation 2), repeat sequence, starting on the left foot
16	repeat continuously, alternating between right foot and left foot

EXERCISE 61: "JUMPS"

Level of difficulty
Grade 1 ↑

Effect and technical characteristics
As an example of how to train *jumps* at beginner levels, outwardly rotated double-footed jumps in the 1st and 2nd position are described below. Legs and feet are completely straight during the flying phase, the landing phase is caught elastically in the *demi plié* position, the torso remains fixed in the straight position throughout.

Starting position: 1st position turned out, arms in neutral position.

cts. Sequence

8	8 *jumps* in 1st position
8	8 *jumps* in 2nd position, arms in 2nd position
8	8 *jumps* alternating between 1st and 2nd position
8	pause
24	repeat sequence

EXERCISE 62: SWINGS

Level of difficulty
Grade 1 ↑

Effect and technical characteristics
This last exercise in the catalogue of exercises describes an example for relaxation after a dance lesson through arm and torso *swings*.

Starting position: standing in 2nd position parallel, arms in 3rd position.

cts.	Sequence	Fig. 85.1-4

cts.	Sequence
2	*swing* arms from outside to inside and upwards (Fig. 85.1)
2	drop bent right arm at the side and *lift* it up again (Fig. 85.2) - drop bent left arm at the side and *lift* it up again (cf. Fig. 85.2)
2	wrap hands quickly over head two times and *swing* arms and torso down deeply in front of body and back up again to half height (Fig. 85.3+4)
2	*swing* arms and torso again down deeply in front of body and *swing* back to full height into starting position repeat sequence several times

85.1   85.2

85.3   85.4

4 JAZZ DANCE TRAINING AT BEGINNER LEVELS

4.1 Didactic-methodical Conception

The following model lessons are meant for beginners who first want to get to know their body as a dance instrument and to increasingly extend its possibilities. Consequently, the focus is not on dancing in choreographic forms but on building up a basic dance training programme.

This Leads to the Following Didactic-methodical Conception

1. Simple basic exercises with which the required stamina and individual technical dance abilities are developed. These basic forms which are demonstrated and explained by the teacher and repeated in every subsequent dance lesson, are the basis for all other forms to follow. They are gradually developed and made more concise, more complex and more demanding. They are also varied with regard to space, tempo, rhythm and dynamics.

2. Floor exercises, because the large support surface allows optimal control and balance work so that incorrect postures can be avoided at the beginning.

3. Working at the barre, where all forms which will later be performed in free space are prepared. Beginners have often not yet learned to stabilize their torso, and coordinating all parts of the body along one single axis is still something new to them. They often have no experience in maintaining balance and still need to familiarize themselves with certain ways of moving. For these dancers the barre offers invaluable help with regard to balance and orientation.

4. Slow execution of the movements, so that the learners can monitor themselves and the teacher has the opportunity to correct them.

5. Musical accompaniment which is appropriate to the form of exercise regarding tempo and dynamics and which does not distract the learner from the movement work itself. At the beginning, the music should help the learner to maintain concentration and to memorize the sequence of the exercises. Only in more advanced classes should it relate to the expressive content of a movement. Further explanations of this are given in the next section.

6. General structure of a 90-minute class at beginner levels 1+2:
   - Centre work 1
   - Floor work 1
   - Barre
   - Floor work 2
   - Isolation
   - Across the floor

The *jazz walks* in the last part of a lesson (Across the floor) are combined as simply as possible at these levels, so that gradually step material is developed for later choreographies. The teacher chooses and arranges the movements for combinations according to the students' current level. Since the subsequent model lessons are only concerned with the development and acquisition of basics, longer combinations based on music are not described.

Each class ends with a relaxation or *release* exercise to balance out the strain.
   The first model lesson is an example for the very first lessons in a beginners' class for amateurs. The second model lesson shows the possible development after six to eight months. Each group will develop at its own pace and within its own range. The guidelines given should therefore not to be regarded as absolute. The overall structure and the exercises of these model lessons correspond with the catalogue of exercises and the teaching methods of ALAIN BERNARD.

4.2 Music and Rhythm in Jazz Dance Training

Jazz Dance cannot exist without music and rhythm. Music is thus used from the very start even in basic *Jazz Dance* training. Since the style of *Jazz Dance* changes with prevailing trends, it is not bound to jazz music. Music of various styles can be used in the lessons.
   It is, however, essential to ensure that newcomers to *Jazz Dance*, who are mainly preoccupied with positioning the parts of their body and with coordinating sequences of movement, are not overstrained and distracted by the music. It is often more appropriate to provide rhythmical accompaniment for an exercise with the voice, in order to underline the timing and the character of an exercise and focus the dancers' concentration more on the performance of the exercises. Simple accompanying rhythms for the exercises produced on drums or other rhythm instruments may also provide better support for the learning process than complex pieces of music.

If music is played via CD or audio cassette, the teacher should be aware of the stimulating and controlling effect of music on movement and choose tracks very carefully so that they correspond with the needs of the beginners.

To sum up: for *Jazz Dance* training at beginner levels, music must first and foremost help the learners to concentrate and to remember the sequence of the movements.

Choice of Music and Use of Music at Beginner Levels

- **General criteria**
- Pieces of pop-, rock- or jazz music with a simple structure.
- Clear, preferably consistent rhythmical structure.
- Catchy, well-known beats, which should not vary within one piece of music (e.g. 2/4, 4/4 or 3/4 beat).
- The musical structure should be easy to recognize and correspond with the sequence of the exercises (e.g.: 4-. 8- or 12 beat groups respectively sequences).
- Dynamic sequences which underline the sequence of the exercises rather than disturbing it through too much or too little power or accentuation.
- Basic tempo and basic mood or character of the music should correspond with the exercise. Thus, for example, a calm, smooth (*legato*) performance of an exercise requires melodic, smooth music, whereas fast, staggered (*staccato*) movements are best underlined by rhythmically accentuated music.
- Too frequent changes of the pieces of music within one lesson or a longer training period have an unfavourable effect. While beginners are still learning the basic abilities, it helps when over a period of time (approximately 2-3 months) certain pieces of music are associated with certain exercises and new stimuli are only introduced through new music when a certain level of technical proficiency has been achieved and the exercises are varied and linked in different ways.
- For technically advanced dancers, the choice of music must be appropriate to the higher demands and the expressiveness of a movement or, to put it the other way round, the forms of exercises must correspond to the expressiveness and the pattern of the music.

- **Beats and counts**

All exercises and sequences of exercises in *Jazz Dance* training are structured in a precise chronological order (see catalogue of exercises and model lessons). This chronological structure is especially suitable for even beats. Odd beats such as

5/4, 7/8 beat and changes of beat or overlapping of different beats should only be used when training advanced students and in choreographies. The counts given do not, however, say anything about the basic tempo or how dynamically the exercises are executed. When choosing music, the following guidelines should be kept in mind:

4/4 rhythm	guided and frozen movements.
2/4 rhythm	accentuated, elastic execution of movements and locomotion.
3/4 rhythm	sweeping movements and waltz steps.

The rhythm and the beats per minute of the music can be associated with the pace of the movement (cf. metronome):

approximately 60-82	slow pace, calm, guided and frozen exercises, corresponds with the musical term *adagio*.
approximately 82-120	medium pace, elastic and accentuated movements, walking pace, corresponds with the musical term *andante*.
approximately 120-165	fast pace, running pace and fast bounces, corresponds with the musical term *moderato and allegro*.

• Music suggestions

The music suggestions and their exemplary assignment to the exercises in *Model Lesson 1* of ALAIN BERNARD were chosen and used by the author. Her experience in the education of students, teachers and trainers is that, at the beginning, they are rather insecure about which kind of music to choose, how to assign it to the exercises and how to use it.

Even though particular pieces of music and singers lose their popularity rapidly, the examples given below should serve as an orientation at the beginning.

Only a selection of tracks from each of the following CDs is given. Other tracks may also be suitable for the lessons. The CDs were chosen according to the following criteria:

- a range of performers with different styles
- the majority of tracks on the CD are suitable for dance training
- the CD offers both calm and rhythmical tracks
- the tracks on the CD have mostly clear musical structures and even rhythms.

4.3 Model Lesson 1

For detailed description of the techniques and functions of the exercises shown in this model lesson, please refer to the catalogue of exercises. The accompanying illustrations correspond to those in the catalogue of exercises and to the standard positions.

4.3.1 Centre Work 1

Exercise 1: "Roll Down and Up"

Effect, technical characteristics and terms
See catalogue of exercises, p. 36.

Starting position: standing in 2nd position parallel, Fig. 86.1.

cts.	Sequence	Fig. 86.1+2
8	roll down and up (Fig. 86.1+2)	
4	roll down and up	
4	roll down and up	
	The sequence of the exercise is subsequently repeated in *2nd position turned out, 1st position parallel and 1st position turned out* with continuous transitions	

Mistakes
- Roll down: insufficient relaxation of the head muscles and the shoulder girdle, fixation of the arms against the legs.
- Roll up: fixation of the arms against the legs, pelvis at first not completely upright, raising the shoulders.

How to correct
- Leave arms hanging freely under the shoulder girdle
- Pause for relaxation after rolling down and let arms and head swing loosely, teacher checks through soft tactile stimuli.

- Practise starts: loosen head and shoulder and straighten up. Straighten up only the pelvis until groin is straight and drop torso again.
- Visualisation: the body is a string of pearls which rolls one pearl after the other down and up.

Examples of music
Phil Collins: "But Seriously", Track 2, 4/4 rhythm, 96 beats.
Note: since every second beat is distinctly emphasised, the exercises can be executed at half speed to start with.
Further suggestions: George Howard, Track 6/ Sidney Youngblood, Track 5 / Annie Lennox, Track 6/ Lionel Ritchie, Track 1/ Shakatak, Track 8.

EXERCISE 2: "FLATBACKS"

Effect, technical characteristics and terms
See catalogue of exercises, p. 38/39.

Starting position: standing, 2nd position parallel, arms in neutral position.

cts.	Sequence	Fig. 87
4	lower straight torso (Fig. 87)	
4	straighten up straight torso	
4	lower straight torso, arms in 2nd position	
4	straighten up torso	
	repeat sequence 3 times	

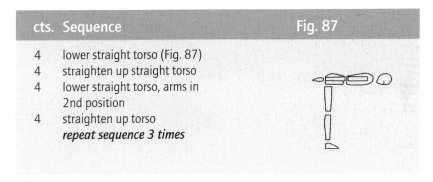

Mistakes
- Rounding the back in the region of the lumbar vertebrae.
- Head not in line with the spine, either too high or too low.
- Bending the knees to compensate for lack of lengthening.

How to correct
- Visualisation: the body is a table on which a glass can stand.
- A stick against the dancer's back, touching it from the coccyx to the back of the head.

- If dancers are not flexible enough in the hip joints and/or do not have enough strength in the muscles of their back, the torso should only be lowered until it reaches a diagonal position.

Examples of music
See Exercise 1: ROLL DOWN AND UP

EXERCISE 3: BEND AND BOUNCES AND PULLS

Effect, technical characteristics and terms
See catalogue of exercises, p.37

Starting position: standing, 2nd position parallel

cts.	Sequence	Fig. 88.1+2
8	bounce deeply 8 times with rounded back (Fig. 88.1)	
8	bounce deeply 8 times with *flat back*, arms in 2nd position (Fig. 88.2) repeat sequence taking 4 and then 2 cts. for each stage	
8	bounce 8 times to the right with straight torso, left arm in 3rd position	
8	bounce 8 times to the left *repeat taking 4 and 2 times 2 cts. for each stage*	

Mistakes
See Exercises 1+2.

How to correct
See Exercises 1+2.

Examples of music
Laid Back: "Hole in the Sky", Track 1, 4/4 rhythm, 128 beats.
Note: the prelude can be fully exploited. Each first beat is distinctly emphasized. The basic tempo is relatively high, each bounce-movement is executed over 2 basic beats, i.e. 2 bounces per beat. Slower paces are also suitable (see below).

Further suggestions: Laid Back, Tracks 2, 3, 5/ Sidney Youngblood, Track 1/ Annie Lennox, Track 2/ Lionel Ritchie, Track 8/ George Howard, Track 1/ Pili Pili, Track 1/ Brent Lewis, Track 3.

4.3.2 Floor Work 1

EXERCISE 4: "FLEXIBILITY OF FEET AND LEGS"

Effect, technical characteristics and terms
See catalogue of exercises, p. 49/50.

Starting position: lying on the back, left leg straight, right knee pulled towards the chest with both hands.

cts.	Sequence	Fig. 89.1+2
8	8 circles of the foot to the outside (Fig. 89.1)	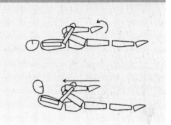
8	8 circles of the foot to the inside	
16	repeat sequence with left foot	
16	pull right and left knee alternately towards chest, and stretch leg again, raising the head (Fig. 89.2)	

Mistakes
• Tension in the shoulder and the neck.
• Incomplete feet circles.

How to correct
• Pull shoulder blades flat onto the floor, make long neck, no double chin.
• Visualisation: feet draw large round circles.

Examples of music
Lionel Ritchie: "Back to the Front", Track 13, 2/4 rhythm, 112 beats.
Note: count at half speed, i.e. one movement for two beats respectively, one beat each.
Further suggestions: George Howard, Track 2/ Phil Collins, Track 7/ Eric Clapton, Tracks 4, 8/ Lionel Ritchie Track 2/ Zaka Percussion, Track 14.

Exercise 5: "Bend and Bounces"

Effect, technical characteristics and terms
See catalogue of exercises, p. 41.

Starting position: sitting up straight, soles of feet against each other.

cts.	Sequence	Fig. 90.1-4
8	bounce rounded torso forwards 8 times, hands next to *pointed* feet (Fig. 90.1)	
8	bounce straight torso forwards 8 times, arms in 1st position (Fig. 90.2)	90.1
4	bounce rounded torso forwards 4 times, hands next to *pointed* feet	
4	bounce straight torso forwards 8 times, arms in 1st position	
8	8 times alternating between rounded torso and straight torso *close and stretch legs*	90.2
8	bounce rounded torso forwards 8 times, hands next to feet (Fig. 90.3)	
8	bounce straight torso forwards 8 times, arms in 1st position, feet *flexed* (Fig. 90.4)	90.3
4	bounce rounded torso forwards 4 times, hands next to *pointed* feet	
4	bounce straight torso forwards 4 times, arms in 1st position, feet are *flexed*	
8	bounce torso forwards 8 times alternating between rounded and straight, *point* feet when torso is round and *flex* feet when torso is straight	90.4

cts. Sequence (continued)   Fig. 90.5-8

Open straight legs into 2nd sitting
position, point feet

8   bounce rounded torso forwards
     8 times (Fig. 90.5)
8   bounce straight torso forwards 8 times,
     flex feet, arms in V-position (Fig. 90.6)
4   bounce rounded torso forwards 4 times
4   bounce straight torso forwards 4 times,
     flex feet, arms in V-position
8   bounce torso forwards 8 times
     alternating between rounded and straight,
     feet alternate between *point* and *flex*
8   bounce upright torso to the right side
     8 times, left arm in 3rd position
     (Fig. 90.7)
4   straighten torso up into neutral position,
     arms in 2nd position
8   bounce upright torso to the left side
     8 times, right arm in 3rd position
     (Fig. 90.8)
4   straighten torso up into neutral position,
     arms in 2nd position
4   bounce upright torso to the right side
     4 times, left arm in 3rd position
2   straighten torso up into neutral position,
     arms in 2nd position
4   bounce upright torso to the left side 4 times,
     right arm in 3rd position
2   straighten torso up into neutral position,
     arms in 2nd position

90.5

90.6

90.7

90.8

Mistakes

- Bending the legs in straight position in order to compensate for lack of lengthening of the muscles of the rear leg and the hip muscles.
- Pulling the shoulders up or forwards.
- Raising the buttocks from the floor.

How to correct
- Work at the point where it is possible with correct posture, not beyond this.
- Heels should not touch the floor (knees cannot bend then).
- Pull shoulder blades downwards towards the spine and fix the arms, only the torso moves from the hip joints onwards.
- Always touch the floor with the ischium (sit on a wand in order to feel this).

Examples of music
Brent Lewis: "Earth Tribe Rhythms", Track 5, 2/4 rhythm, 128 beats.
Note: percussions, instrumental, execute one bounce-movement over two beats.
Further suggestions: see Exercise 3: "BEND AND BOUNCE"

EXERCISE 6: "PLIÉS"

Effect, technical characteristics and terms
See catalogue of exercises, p. 47/48.

Starting position: sitting with open legs (2nd position), hands support backwards on fingertips.

cts.	Sequence	Fig. 91.1+2
4	right leg *plié* and stretch (Fig. 91.1)	
4	left leg *plié* and stretch	
8	repeat	
4	both legs *plié* and stretch (Fig. 91.2)	
4	repeat	
	repeat whole sequence starting with the left leg	

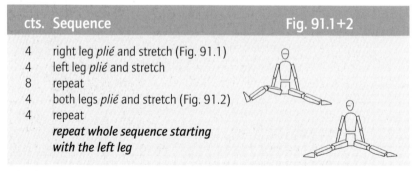

Mistakes
- Body bends backwards, shoulders are pulled up.
- Knees and legs are not aligned one above the other.

How to correct
- Note: press upwards from the floor and pull shoulders downwards.
- Help: lean against a wall.
- Dancers execute movement very slowly while watching themselves.
- Visualisation: elastic band runs from toes to knee and shortens and lengthens in a straight line. Knee and foot bend and stretch within a "rail".

Examples of music
See Exercise 4: "FLEXIBILITY OF FEET AND LEGS"

EXERCISE 7: BREATHINGS

Effect, technical characteristics and terms
See catalogue of exercises, p. 44.

Starting position: sitting with crossed legs, back rounded, arms rest on knees, face straight ahead (Fig. 92.1).

cts.	Sequence	Fig. 92.1-4
4	straighten up torso, inhale (Fig. 92.2)	
4	back into starting position, exhale	
4	while straightening up torso *lift* head and sternum (Fig. 92.3)	
4	starting position	
4	straighten up torso with *lift* and arm gesture (Fig. 92.4)	
4	starting position	
	change legs with arms in 2nd position	
2	straighten up and stretch right leg	
2	stretch left leg	
2	lock right leg in	
2	lock left leg in	
4	bring torso back into starting position and exhale	
	repeat whole sequence starting with the other leg.	

92.1   *92.2*

92.3   *92.4*

Mistakes
• Not starting the movement with shift of the centre of gravity either forwards upwards or backwards downwards.
• Pulling the shoulders up instead of raising the chest.
• Torso collapses during change of legs.

How to correct
• Practise starts and show how to shift the centre of gravity forwards and backwards, e.g. while sitting on a thin wand.

- Visualisation: widen chest like an air balloon and raise sternum, drop shoulders simultaneously.
- Support backwards on the fingers in case not enough holding power has been developed yet.

Examples of music
Annie Lennox: "Diva", Track 1, 4/4 rhythm, 92 beats.
Further suggestions: Eric Clapton, Tracks 4, 8/ Lionel Ritchie, Tracks 11, 15/ Phil Collins, Tracks 3, 9.

EXERCISE 8: "CONTRACTIONS"

Effect, technical characteristics and terms
See catalogue of exercises, p. 51.

Starting position: upright knee sit, arms straight in front of body, hands holding ankles.

cts.	Sequence	Fig. 93.1+2

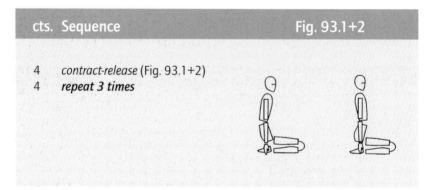

| 4 | *contract-release* (Fig. 93.1+2) |
| 4 | *repeat 3 times* |

Mistakes
- Lumbar vertebrae not rounded enough and pelvis not tilted far enough backwards.
- Bending the torso forwards and pulling the shoulder girdle together.

How to correct
- Do an exercise lying on the back first (see sequence of exercises *"Contraction"*).
- Visualisation: an elastic band which shortens and lengthens vertically connects shoulder joint and hip joint.

Examples of music
Sidney Youngblood: "Feeling Free", Track 1, 4/4 rhythm, 118 beats.
Note: the exercises are executed at half the speed of the music, i.e. 1 movement over 2 beats.
Further suggestions: Pili Pili, Tracks 1, 9/ Shakatak, Track 4/ Laid Back, Tracks 3, 5/ Eric Clapton, Track 10/ Zaka Percussion, Track 14.

4.3.3 Barre

The illustrations are from the catalogue of exercises and so there is no barre in some of the figures.

EXERCISE 9: "FLAT BACK"

Effect, technical characteristics and terms
See catalogue of exercises, p. 65.

Starting position: standing facing the barre, 2nd position parallel, hands hold the barre at shoulder width, torso and legs are at an angle of 90 degrees (Fig. 94.1).

cts.	Sequence	Fig. 94.1+2
4	shift torso forwards until elbows are under the shoulder girdle, head is under the barre (Fig. 94.2)	
4	back into starting position	
8	bounce torso deeply, side of little finger rests on the barre	
	repeat sequence 3 times	

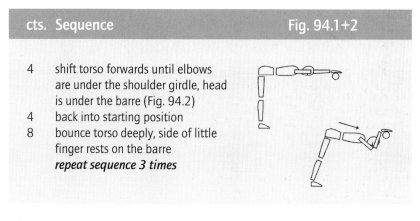

Mistakes
• Lifting the elbows up sideways, head in the nape of the neck.

How to correct
• Shift elbows towards the wall, hook into elbows, pull neck long.

Examples of music
Phil Collins: "But Seriously", Track 3, 4/4 rhythm, 92 beats
Further suggestions: Phil Collins, Track 9/ Lionel Ritchie, Track 3/ Laid Back, Tracks 4, 8.

EXERCISE 10: "BOUNCING PLIÉS"

Effect, technical characteristics and terms
See catalogue of exercises, p.55.

Starting position: 1st position parallel, standing facing the barre, hands hold the barre.

cts.	Sequence	Fig. 95
8	8 leg bounces (*pliés*)	
8	repeat in 1st position turned out	
8	repeat in 2nd position parallel	
8	repeat in 2nd position turned out	
	(Fig. 95)	

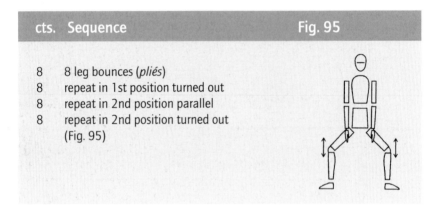

Mistakes
- Shifting the pelvis backwards.
- Knees fall inwards in the outwardly rotated positions, weight over inner edge of the foot.

How to correct
- To build up the posture try upright position of the pelvis with bent legs against the wall.
- Bounce the knees more towards the little toe and pull up the plantar arch consciously (this foot exercise might be done in preparation).

Examples of music
See Exercise 3: "BEND AND BOUNCE" and Exercise 5: "BOUNCES".

EXERCISE 11: PLIÉS

Effect, technical characteristics and terms
See catalogue of exercises, p. 56.

Starting position: standing facing the barre, 1st position turned out, both hands hold the barre.

cts.	Sequence	Fig. 96.1-3

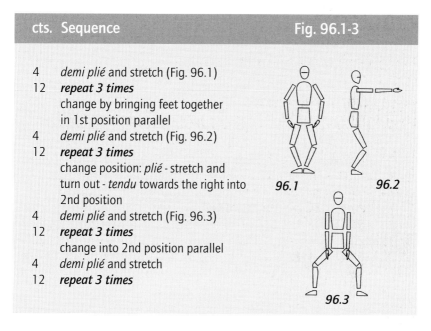

4	*demi plié* and stretch (Fig. 96.1)
12	*repeat 3 times*
	change by bringing feet together in 1st position parallel
4	*demi plié* and stretch (Fig. 96.2)
12	*repeat 3 times*
	change position: *plié* - stretch and turn out - *tendu* towards the right into 2nd position
4	*demi plié* and stretch (Fig. 96.3)
12	*repeat 3 times*
	change into 2nd position parallel
4	*demi plié* and stretch
12	*repeat 3 times*

96.1   *96.2*

96.3

Mistakes
- Incorrect posture, see Exercise 10.
- No continuity in rhythmical-dynamic sequence resulting in a pause at the point of return.

How to correct
- Use of the imagination to develop counter tension: when bending the knees, "knees and body stretch upwards", "touch the ceiling"; when stretching the knees "press into the floor", "grow out of the floor".

Examples of music
See Exercise 9: "FLAT BACK".

EXERCISE 12: "STRETCHING, LEG ON BARRE"

Effect, technical characteristics and terms
See catalogue of exercises, p. 74.

Starting position: standing facing the barre, legs are parallel, right middle foot rests on the barre with the knee bent, hands hold the barre next to the foot, rounded torso is on the thigh (Fig. 97.1).

cts.	Sequence	Fig. 97.1+2

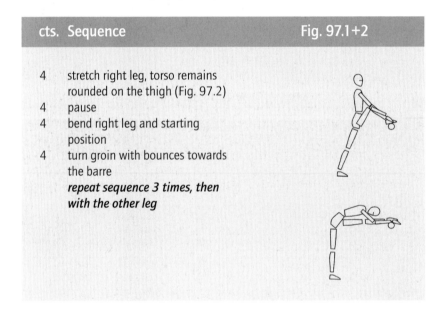

cts.	Sequence
4	stretch right leg, torso remains rounded on the thigh (Fig. 97.2)
4	pause
4	bend right leg and starting position
4	turn groin with bounces towards the barre
	repeat sequence 3 times, then with the other leg

Mistakes
• The pelvis moves through turn towards the supporting leg.
• Bending the supporting leg.

How to correct
• Build up posture through verbal and tactile correction.
• If the dancer is not flexible enough, choose lower barre.

Examples of music
Lionel Ritchie: "Back to the Front", Track 15, 4/4 rhythm, 64 beats.
Further suggestions: Lionel Ritchie, Tracks 3, 11/ George Howard, Track 3/ Annie Lennox, Track 10.

EXERCISE 13: "BEND AND BOUNCE"

Effect, technical characteristics and terms
See catalogue of exercises, p. 75.

Starting position: right side faces barre, right leg bent on the barre, middle foot rests on the barre, right hand holds the barre in front of the right foot.

cts.	Sequence	Fig. 98.1+2

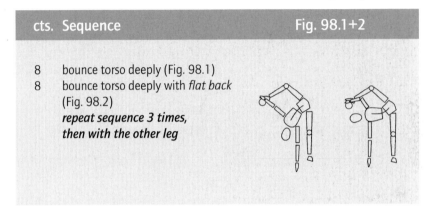

8   bounce torso deeply (Fig. 98.1)
8   bounce torso deeply with *flat back*
    (Fig. 98.2)
    repeat sequence 3 times,
    then with the other leg

Mistakes
• Back not stretched far enough in the *flat back* position.
• Bending the supporting leg.

How to correct
• Achieve extended position through support of one hand on the thigh.
• Ensure the right height of the barre.

Examples of music
Brent Lewis: "Earth Tribe Rhythms", Track 6, 2/4 rhythm, 96 beats.
Further suggestions: see Exercise 8: "CONTRACTIONS".

EXERCISE 14: "LEG FORTIFICATION"

Effect, technical characteristics and terms
See catalogue of exercises, p. 69.

Starting position: standing facing the barre in 2nd position turned out, hands hold the barre.

cts.	Sequence	Fig. 99.1+2
4	*demi plié*	
4	bounce deeply 4 times (Fig. 99.1)	
4	bend right leg	
4	bounce 4 times (Fig. 99.2)	
4	bend both legs in the centre	
4	stretch both legs	
	repeat sequence for the other side and then each side again	

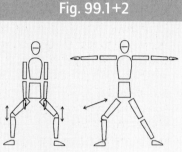

Mistakes
See Exercises 10 and 11.

How to correct
See Exercises 10 and 11.

Examples of music
See Exercise 8: "CONTRACTIONS".

EXERCISE 15: "LEG SWINGS"

Effect, technical characteristics and terms
See catalogue of exercises, p. 64/65.

Starting position: stand with back towards the barre on outwardly rotated left leg, right side *tendu*, hands hold on to the barre sideways.

cts.	Sequence	Fig. 100.1+2
8	bent right leg *swings* forwards then sideways 4 times through 1st position turned out, integrate shift of weight with *plié* (Fig. 100.1+2)	
8	bent left leg *swings* forwards then sideways 4 times through 1st position *turned* out	
16	*repeat sequence with the right leg and with the left leg*	

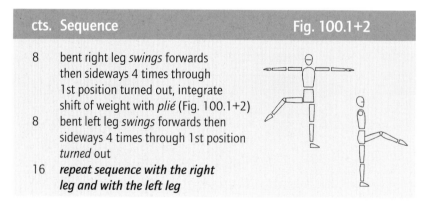

Mistakes
* 1st position is not brushed through on the whole sole of the foot.
* Leg is *turned* in when *swinging* forwards.
* Hip is raised when *swinging* sideways, in order to *swing* the leg higher.
* The hip of the supporting leg is moved towards the side.

How to correct
* Demonstrate movement of the leg very slowly and consciously in all individual phases and practise.
* Do not *swing* the leg up higher than is possible with upright pelvis position, give tactile help.
* Demonstrate how to fix the hip: move hip of the supporting leg to one side (drop) and draw the leg consciously inwards on the supporting surface of the whole foot; hold the tension (abductors) and let free leg swing loosely with the hip fixed.

Examples of music
Brent Lewis: "Earth Tribe Rhythms", Track 3, 3/4 rhythm, 192 basic beats (64 bars).
Note: one leg swing per beat, very fast tempo.
Further suggestions: Tracks 3,5 (slow tempo).

4.3.4 Floor Work 2

EXERCISE 16: "ROLL UP AND DOWN"

Effect, technical characteristics and terms
See catalogue of exercises, p. 87.

Starting position: lying on the back, feet are flat on the floor, arms are next to the body.

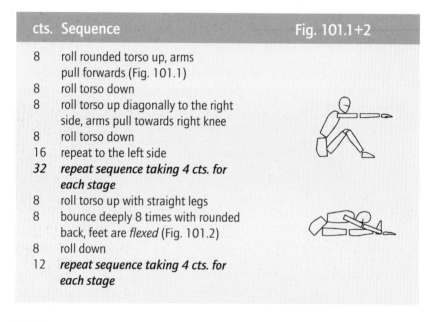

cts.	Sequence	Fig. 101.1+2
8	roll rounded torso up, arms pull forwards (Fig. 101.1)	
8	roll torso down	
8	roll torso up diagonally to the right side, arms pull towards right knee	
8	roll torso down	
16	repeat to the left side	
32	*repeat sequence taking 4 cts. for each stage*	
8	roll torso up with straight legs	
8	bounce deeply 8 times with rounded back, feet are *flexed* (Fig. 101.2)	
8	roll down	
12	*repeat sequence taking 4 cts. for each stage*	

Mistakes
- Pulling the shoulders up forwards.
- *Lifting* the feet off the floor when rolling up, when the bending phase of the spine is finished and the *flexing* phase of the hips starts.
- Torso "falls backwards" onto the floor with straight lumbar vertebrae when rolling down.

How to correct
- Fix the shoulder blades backwards and downwards, "Torso executes the movement".

- Lack of strength and bending flexibility of the lumbar vertebrae might be the reason for the problem. The following exercises might help: partner holds the feet down. Roll up to the waist only, hold torso in this position or bounce, roll down. Hold one knee with both hands, roll up and down pressing the knee against the hands.

Examples of music
See Exercise 4: "FLEXIBILITY OF FEET AND LEGS".

EXERCISE 17: "LEG WORK BACK"

Effect, technical characteristics and terms
See catalogue of exercises, p. 86.

Starting position: lying on the stomach, forehead rests on the hands.

cts.	Sequence	Fig. 102.1-3
4	3 cts. *lift* right leg up - 1 ct. lower leg (Fig. 102.1)	
4	repeat with left leg	
4	repeat with both legs	
4	repeat with both legs	
	Starting position: lift upper body up and support on forearms	
4	3 cts. lift right leg up - 1 ct. lower leg	
4	repeat with left leg	
8	*lift* bent right leg up 7 times - 1 ct. stretch and lower leg (Fig. 102.2)	
8	repeat with left leg	
8	*lift* up legs, torso and arms and hold (Fig. 102.3)	
4	lower	
4	to relax place rounded torso onto thighs in knee sit	

102.1

102.2

102.3

Mistakes
- Raising the pelvis when the torso is lying on the floor in order to be able to *lift* the leg up higher.
- Pushing the shoulders up when torso is supported.

How to correct
- Give verbal help: the pelvis bones must always remain in contact with the floor.
- Stretch your neck, press straight torso against the floor.

Examples of music
Brent Lewis: "Earth Tribe Rhythms", Track 1, 4/4 rhythm, 128 beats.
Further suggestions: Pili Pili, Tracks 1,9/ Shakatak, Track 4/ Laid Back, Tracks 3,5/ Eric Clapton, Track 10/ Zaka Percussion, Track 14.

Exercise 18: "Battements"

Effect, technical characteristics and terms
See catalogue of exercises, p. 92.

Starting position: lying on the back, legs are straight and closed, arms are on the floor in 2nd position.

cts.	Sequence	Fig. 103.1+2
4	*battements* forwards and upwards with right leg (Fig. 103.1)	
4	change into lying on the left side, legs *turned* out and closed, head rests on straight left arm, right arm supports in front of the chest	
8	4 *battements* sideways with right leg (Fig. 103.2)	
4	change into lying on the stomach, forehead rests on the hands	

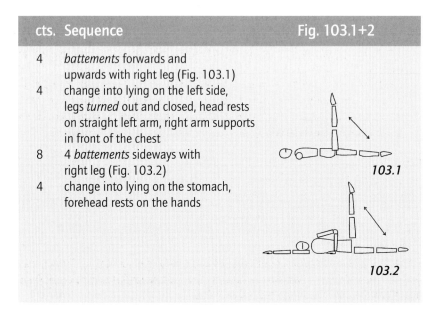

103.1

103.2

cts.	Sequence (continued)	Fig. 103.3
8	4 *battements* backwards with right leg (Fig. 103.3)	
4	change into lying on the right side, legs turned out and closed, head rests on straight right arm, left arm supports in front of the chest	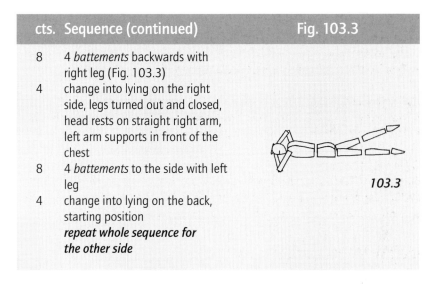
8	4 *battements* to the side with left leg	*103.3*
4	change into lying on the back, starting position **repeat whole sequence for the other side**	

Mistakes

• Raising the pelvis when doing the *battement* forwards and upwards and slight bend of the lying leg.

• Rolling back the pelvis and bending the groin when doing the *battement* to the side, tensing the shoulder girdle.

How to correct

• Thrust leg up only as far as possible with the pelvis fixed on the floor and the leg kept straight; work on this point.

• The body is very unstable when lying on the side, so this position must be practised constantly through posture and tension exercises. Visualisation: the weight is placed a little bit in front of the hips, the body makes one single straight line from head to toe.

Examples of music

See Exercise 17: "LEG WORK BACK".

4.3.5 Isolation

For technical characteristics, terms, figures and photos see section 3.2 "Functional Basics" and section 3.4 "Catalogue of Exercises". The examples of music are given here at the beginning for all isolation exercises.

Examples of music
Pili Pili: "Stolen Moments", Track 9, 4/4 rhythm, 88 beats.
Note: This piece of music is very rhythmical and has a slow basic beat, so that the isolations can be executed *staccato* and with control. For faster examples of music see below.
Further suggestions: Sidney Youngblood, Tracks 2,7/ Pili Pili, Track 6/ Zaka Percussion, Tracks 1,7/ Annie Lennox, Track 4/ Eric Clapton, Track 6/ Brent Lewis, Tracks 1,6.

EXERCISE 19: "HEAD ISOLATION"

cts. Starting position: 2nd position parallel, hands touch the groin

Sequence

8	*turn* head to the right side 2 times - neutral position - left - neutral position
8	lower head 2 times - neutral position - *lift* - neutral position
8	bend head 2 times to the right side - neutral position - bend head to the left side - neutral position
8	nod head 2 times to the right side - neutral position - left - neutral position
8	2 head circles going from the right side - backwards - to the left side - forwards
8	2 head circles starting on the left side

Mistakes
• Planes are not maintained.
• Head circles go too far backwards.

How to correct
• Fix exact points to look at when turning the head, use the mirror. Possibly floor exercise, head slides on the floor. Tactile correction.
• Note: pull neck long and execute minor movement backwards.

EXERCISE 20: SHOULDER ISOLATION

cts.	Starting position: 2nd position parallel, arms in 2nd jazz position

Sequence

8	raise and lower right shoulder 4 times
8	raise and lower left shoulder 4 times
8	raise and lower both shoulders 4 times
8	raise and lower right shoulder and left shoulder alternately 8 times
8	*shift* right shoulder forwards and backwards 4 times
8	*shift* left shoulder forwards and backwards 4 times
8	*shift* both shoulders forwards and backwards 4 times
8	*shift* right shoulder and left shoulder forwards and backwards alternately 4 times
8	4 shoulder circles backwards with the right shoulder
8	4 shoulder circles backwards with the left shoulder
8	4 shoulder circles backwards with both shoulders
8	4 shoulder circles forwards with the right shoulder
8	4 shoulder circles forwards with the left shoulder
8	4 shoulder circles forwards with both shoulders

Mistakes
- Moving the chest along in all these directions.

How to correct
- Fix body by touch, use mirror.

EXERCISE 21: "CHEST ISOLATION"

cts.	Starting position: 2nd position parallel, hands touch the groin

Sequence

8	*shift* chest 2 times to the right side - neutral position - left - neutral position
8	*shift* chest forwards 2 times - neutral position - backwards - neutral position
8	*shift* chest forwards - to the right side - backwards - to the left side

Mistakes
- Bending the upper body towards one side.
- Moving the pelvis while executing the exercise.
- Pulling the shoulder girdle forwards and backwards.

How to correct
- When moving the arms to the sides in 2nd position: hold arms and shoulder girdle in horizontal axis.
- Fix pelvis by touch; triangle of the legs must remain isosceles.
- Clarify starting points by "comparing".

EXERCISE 22: "PELVIS ISOLATION"

cts. Starting position: 2nd position parallel, arms in neutral position

Sequence

8	*shift* pelvis to the right 2 times - neutral position - to the left - neutral position
8	*shift* pelvis alternately to the right side and to the left side 4 times
8	*contract* pelvis 2 times - neutral position - *release* - neutral position
8	alternate between *contract* - *release* 4 times

Mistakes
- Moving the upper body along in all directions.
- *Shifting* the weight from one leg over the other.

How to correct
- Correct with the help of the mirror.
- Arms in 2nd position, hold in horizontal axis.
- Close eyes and concentrate on distributing the weight evenly over both feet.

EXERCISE 23: "HAND ISOLATION"

cts.	Starting position: 2nd position parallel, arms extended forwards

Sequence

8	8 hand circles outside to the right side
8	8 hand circles outside to the left side
8	8 hand circles inside to the right side
8	8 hand circles inside to the left side
8	spread hand and make fist 8 times, alternating between right hand and left hand
8	spread both hands and make fist 8 times

EXERCISE 24: "BRUSHES"

cts.	Starting position: 1st position parallel, arms in neutral position	Fig. 104.1-3

Sequence

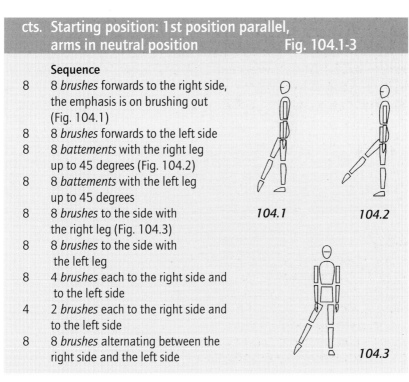

8	8 *brushes* forwards to the right side, the emphasis is on brushing out (Fig. 104.1)
8	8 *brushes* forwards to the left side
8	8 *battements* with the right leg up to 45 degrees (Fig. 104.2)
8	8 *battements* with the left leg up to 45 degrees
8	8 *brushes* to the side with the right leg (Fig. 104.3)
8	8 *brushes* to the side with the left leg
8	4 *brushes* each to the right side and to the left side
4	2 *brushes* each to the right side and to the left side
8	8 *brushes* alternating between the right side and the left side

104.1

104.2

104.3

Mistakes
- Bending of the knee and foot is "set out".
- Hip of the supporting leg *"falls"* outwards.

How to correct
- Tense the thigh stretchers as fast as possible and *"lift* up the kneecap".
- Fix the hip, see Exercise 15.

4.3.6 Across the Floor

In the catalogue of exercises and the model lessons according to ALAIN BERNARD, only a few basic *jazz walks* and ways of varying and combining them are presented, since this is the zone of transition from basic dance training proper and stylistic artistic design.

How teachers and trainers handle these techniques in locomotion depends to a great degree on how much basic and further education in the area of *Jazz Dance* they received, and on their imagination and musicality. Thus suggestions of possible mistakes are not provided here. A few examples of music are mentioned before the descriptions of the *jazz walks*.

Examples of music
Shakatak: "Turn the Music up", Tracks 1,2,7,10,12, 4/4 rhythm, 112-128 beats.

Note: These pieces of music belong to the categories of Jazz-Rock and Latin dance. Their walking tempo ranges from medium to fast.

Eric Clapton: "Unplugged", Tracks 2,6,7,10, 2/4 and 4/4 rhythm, 100-105 beats.

Note: These pieces of music contain elements of Blues and Pop and their walking tempo ranges from slow to medium.

Zaka Percussion: "Le Chant du Monde", Tracks 1,2,11, 2/4 and 4/4 rhythm, 118-135 beats.

Note: These pieces of music are particularly appropriate for bounced movements in the Latin American style. Their walking tempo ranges from slow over medium to fast bouncing tempo.

Exercise 25: Step-Tip

cts. Sequence

cts.	
1	one step forwards on the right foot, ball of foot is placed on the floor first, leg is straight
1	toe *tip* of left foot is placed next to ball of right foot, with no weight over the left foot: *tip*
1	one step forwards on the left foot, ball of foot is placed on the floor first, leg is straight
1	toe *tip* of right foot is placed next to ball of left foot, with no weight over the right foot: *tip* repeat continuously

cts. Variation

cts.	
2	step on the right foot - *tip* with the left foot (cf. sequence of movement)
2	step on the left foot - *tip* with the right foot
4	step forwards on the right foot - backwards on the left foot - backwards on the right foot - forwards on the left foot with each step slight *turn* of the hip repeat continuously, then start on the left foot

Exercise 26: Contraction Walk

Starting position: weight over the left foot with *demi plié*, right ball next to left foot with no weight on right ball.

cts. Sequence   Fig. 105.1+2

cts.	
1	place right foot forwards through *contraction*, put all weight over right foot, left foot is on balls (Fig.105.1)
1	*release* (Fig. 105.2)
1	place left foot forwards through *contraction*, put all weight over left foot, left foot on balls
1	*release* repeat continuously

Exercise 27: "Side Walk with Leg Rotation"

Starting position: weight over left foot with *demi plié*, right ball next to left foot with no weight over right ball.

cts.	Sequence	Fig. 106
1	step to the right side parallel in *plié* sideways by taking off on left heel, with outward rotation of left leg (Fig. 106)	
1	step to the left side parallel in *plié* next to right leg repeat continuously in the direction of the movement, first to the right side, then to the left side	

Exercise 28: "Side Walk with Hip Shift"

cts.	Sequence	Fig. 107
1	step to the right side parallel in *plié* sideways by taking off on left ball, with hip *shift* to the left side (Fig. 107, here with simultaneous head and chest isolation *polycentrics)*.	
1	bring left foot parallel next to right foot, with the weight over the ball, with hip *shift* to the right side repeat continuously, then for the other side with change of direction, over 4 and 2 steps	

Exercise 29: "Swings"

Starting position: standing, 2nd position parallel, arms in 3rd position.

cts.	Sequence	Fig. 108.1-4
2	2 arm circles from the outside to the inside upwards (Fig. 108.1)	
2	drop right arm bent sideways and raise it again (Fig. 108.2) - drop left arm bent sideways and raise it again (cf. Fig. 108.2)	
2	wrap hands fast 2 times over the head and *swing* arms with torso forwards - deeply and shoulder high (Fig. 108.3+4)	
2	*swing* arms again forwards deeply and then up high into starting position repeat sequence several times	

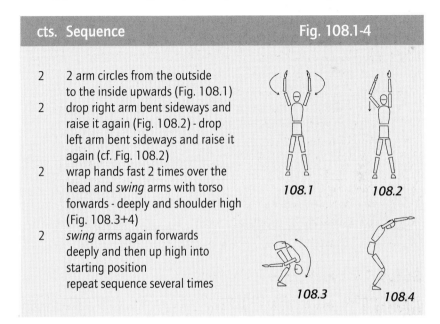

108.1   *108.2*

108.3   *108.4*

4.4 Model Lesson 2

The catalogue of exercises provides detailed descriptions of the *techniques and effects* of the exercises listed below. The illustrations and photos correspond with those of the *catalogue of exercises* and with the standard positions and have been assigned to the sequences of the exercises once more to make work easier. *Examples of music and possible mistakes with suggestions on how to correct them* are mostly to be found under *Model Lesson 1*. They have been added here only if a completely new technique is dealt with.

Exercises which are identical with the ones from Model Lesson 1 are here only referred to by their title. To provide a quick survey of the exercises, all variations of exercises with regard to their sequence, rhythm, or number or newly incorporated exercises are marked with an **asterisk*. The more complex *techniques are underlined*.

4.4.1 Centre Work 1

EXERCISE 1: "ROLL DOWN AND UP"

Sequence
Cf. Model Lesson 1, p. 124.

EXERCISE 2: "FLATBACKS"

Starting position: standing 2nd position parallel, arms in neutral position

cts.	Sequence	Fig. 109.1-4
4	bend the straight torso (Fig.109.1)	
4	bring straight torso into upright position	
8	repeat	109.1
4	bend the straight torso, arms in 2nd position (Fig. 109.2)	
4	bring straight torso into upright position	
8	repeat	109.2
4	*bend torso, arms in 3rd position	
4	straighten up torso	
8	repeat	
4	bend torso	
4	plié (Fig. 109.3)	109.3
4	stretch legs	
4	straighten up torso	
4	*flat back back bend (Fig. 109.4)	
4	straighten up	
24	repeat	109.4

Mistakes
* Rounding the back in *plié* position.
* Lordosis in *flat back back bend* position.

How to correct
* Do not lower the buttocks when bending the legs, "stretch the buttocks outwards backwards".
* With the pelvis forwards shift the weight over the feet, *lift* upper body far up high first and then bend backwards to avoid putting weight incorrectly onto the lumbar vertebrae. Tense the abdominals!

EXERCISE 3: "BEND AND BOUNCE"

Starting position: standing, 2nd position parallel.

cts.	Sequence	Fig. 110.1-3

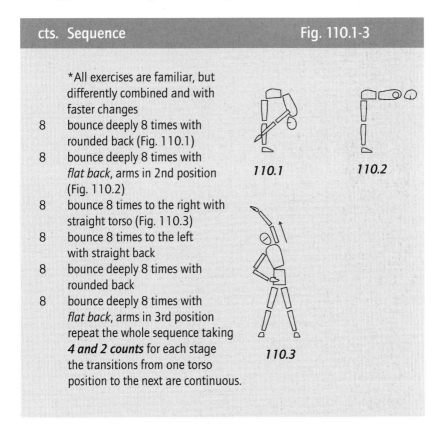

	*All exercises are familiar, but differently combined and with faster changes
8	bounce deeply 8 times with rounded back (Fig. 110.1)
8	bounce deeply 8 times with *flat back*, arms in 2nd position (Fig. 110.2)
8	bounce 8 times to the right with straight torso (Fig. 110.3)
8	bounce 8 times to the left with straight back
8	bounce deeply 8 times with rounded back
8	bounce deeply 8 times with *flat back*, arms in 3rd position repeat the whole sequence taking **4 and 2 counts** for each stage the transitions from one torso position to the next are continuous.

110.1   *110.2*

110.3

EXERCISE 4: "LATERALS"

Starting position: standing, large 2nd position parallel, arms in V-position.

cts.	Sequence	Fig. 111.1+2
	*Technique and sequence are new.	
4	hip *shift* to the left and *laterals* to the right (Fig. 111.1+2)	
4	straighten up into neutral position	
4	hip *shift* to the right and *laterals* to the left	
4	straighten up into neutral position	
16	repeat the *laterals* at slow speed	
8	repeat the *laterals* two times to the right and to the left at fast speed	
	repeat the whole sequence	

Mistakes
- Tilting the pelvis forwards with lordosis.
- Turning the torso and the head out of the frontal plane.
- Raising the shoulders and shifted V-position of the arms.

How to correct
- Tense the abdominals and the buttocks tightly, pull the groin long.
- Visualisation: execute the *laterals* between two narrow walls.
- Exercise: raise the shoulders "towards the ears" with lifted arms, then pull down consciously, arms remain straight.
- Visualisation: the torso moves, not the arms, the head is and remains the centre of a "piece of pie".

EXERCISE 5: "LATERALS AND FLAT BACK"

Starting position: standing, large 2nd position parallel.

cts.	Sequence	Fig. 112.1+2
	*Technique and sequence are new.	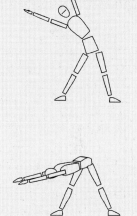
4	hip *shift* to the left and *lateral* flexion to the right (Fig. 112.1)	
4	rotation into *flat back* diagonally forwards to the right (Fig. 112.2)	
4	rotation back into *lateral* flexion to the right (cf. Fig.112.1)	
4	straighten up into neutral position	
4	hip *shift* to the right and *lateral* flexion to the left	
4	rotation into *flat back* diagonally forwards to the left	
4	rotation back into *lateral* flexion to the left	
4	straighten up into neutral position **repeat whole sequence to the right and to the left**	

Mistakes

- Incomplete *turn* of the upper body towards the floor.
- *Shift* of the weight towards the side where the torso is and inward rotation of the opposite leg.
- Lack of pelvis straightening when rotating into the laterals.

How to correct

- Tactile correction.
- Note: press the opposite leg hard into the floor.
- *Shift* the pelvis forwards first and straighten it up, upper body follows.

4.4.2 Floor Work 1

EXERCISE 6: "FLEXIBILITY OF FEET AND LEGS"

Starting position: lying on the back, right knee pulled against the breast with both hands.

cts.	Sequence	Fig. 113.1+2
8	8 foot circles outwards (Fig.113.1)	
8	8 foot circles inwards	
4	*pull knee outwards, left arm in 2nd position	
4	pull knee against the breast and change hands	
4	*pull knee inwards, right arm in 2nd position	
4	pull knee against the breast, hold with both hands	
8	bounce knee 8 times towards the breast	
2	put leg down	
2	bend left leg and pull against the breast	
	repeat sequence with the left leg	
16	pull right knee and left knee alternately against the breast 16 times and stretch again, raising the head (Fig. 113.2)	

Mistakes
- Lifting the opposite hip when rolling out.
- *Shifting* the lying leg out of the vertical axis when rolling in.

How to correct
- Press hip hard into floor by way of counter pull, hand on groin helps to reinforce the downward pressure.
- Draw a line from head to toe.
- Visualisation: the lying leg is the "supporting" leg, it cannot escape.

EXERCISE 7: "BOUNCES AND ISOLATION"

Starting Position: sitting in upright position, foot-soles together.

cts. Sequence

Fig. 114.1+2

8	bounce rounded torso forwards 8 times (Fig.114.1)
8	bounce straight torso forwards 8 times, arms in 1st position (Fig 114.2)
8	bounce forwards 8 times alternating between rounded and straight torso
8	*shift chest 8 times to the right and to the left in upright position, arms in 2nd position

change of position: stretch and close legs for 1st position

cts. Sequence (continued)

Fig. 115.1+2

8	bounce rounded torso forwards 8 times
8	bounce straight torso forwards 8 times, arms in 1st position, feet are *flexed*
8	bounce 8 times alternating between rounded and straight torso
8	*shift* chest 8 times in upright position to the right and to the left, arms in 2nd position

change of position: open straight legs for 2nd sitting position

115.1

8	bounce rounded torso forwards 8 times
8	bounce straight torso forwards 8 times, arms in V-position, *flex* feet
8	bounce 8 times alternating between rounded and straight torso, and between pointed and *flexed* feet (see above)
8	*shift* chest 8 times in upright position to the right and to the left, arms in 2nd position
8	bounce rounded torso 8 times over right leg (Fig. 115.1)

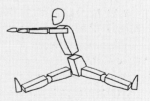

115.2

cts.	Sequence (continued)	Fig. 115.3-4

8	bounce straight torso 8 times over right leg, arms in 1st position, feet are *flexed* (Fig. 115.2)	
8	bounce 8 times alternating between rounded and straight torso, and between *pointed* and *flexed* feet	
24	repeat sequence over the left leg	
8	*shift* chest 8 times in upright position forwards and backwards	
8	bounce straight torso 8 times to the right side, left arm in 3rd position (Fig. 115.3)	*115.3*
2	back into neutral position, arms in 2nd position	
8	bounce straight torso 8 times to the left side, right arm in 3rd position (Fig. 115.4)	
2	straighten up into neutral position, arms in 2nd position	
4	bounce torso 4 times to the right, left arm in 3rd position	
2	straighten up torso, arms in 2nd position	
4	bounce torso 4 times to the left, right arm in 3rd position	*115.4*
2	straighten up torso, lower the arms	

Mistakes
- Pelvis not straightened up well enough, *shifting* the weight and tilting the shoulder girdle to one side during the isolation.

How to correct
- You might try out the movement sitting against a wall, both ischia remain in contact with the floor throughout. Tactile help (see also Model Lesson 1, Exercise 21).

EXERCISE 8: "PLIÉS"

Starting position: sitting with open legs (2nd position), *arms in neutral position.

cts.	Sequence	Fig. 116.1+2
4	right leg *plié* and stretch, right arm moves forwards then up and outwards, face to the right hand (Fig. 116.1+2)	
4	left leg *plié* and stretch, left arm moves forwards then up and outwards, face to the left hand	
8	repeat	
4	both legs *plié* and stretch, open both arms over the head, torso and face in neutral position	
4	repeat	

Mistakes
• Raising the shoulders when moving the arms.

How to correct
• Visualisation: arms are *lifted* up through pull of the shoulder blades downwards.

EXERCISE 9: "BREATHINGS"

Starting position: sitting cross-legged, back rounded, arms on the knees, face forwards (Fig. 117.1)

cts.	Sequence	Fig. 117.1-3

4	straighten up torso, inhale
4	back to starting position, exhale
4	straighten up torso with *lift* of sternum and head
4	starting position
4	straighten up torso with *lift* and arm movement (Fig. 117.2)
4	starting position
4	*straighten up torso, inhale
4	rotate right side forwards, face to the right across the forward shoulder, exhale (Fig. 117.3)
4	rotate back to starting position, inhale
4	starting position, exhale
16	*repeat with rotation to the left, and back to starting position

117.1   *117.2*

117.3

cts.	Sequence (continued)	Fig. 118.1+2

change legs with arms in 2nd position

2	straighten up torso while stretching the right leg through rotation of the torso with the right side forwards, face to the right (Fig. 118.1)
2	stretch the left leg through rotation of the torso with the left side forwards, face to the left
2	lock right leg in through rotation of the torso with the left side backwards, face to the right (Fig. 118.2)
2	lock left leg in through rotation of the torso with the right side backwards, face to the left
4	turn torso into neutral position and back to starting position, exhale
	repeat whole sequence for the other side

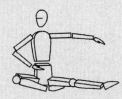

Mistakes
• Instead of *turning* the torso, pulling one shoulder forwards.

How to correct
• Visualisation: torso *turns* forwards with the right side through pull of the left shoulder blade backwards. Tactile correction.

EXERCISE 10: "CONTRACTIONS"

Starting position: upright knee sit, arms extended in front of the body, hands holding ankles.

cts.	Sequence	Fig. 119.1-3

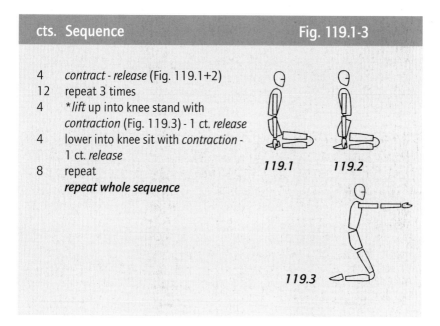

4	*contract - release* (Fig. 119.1+2)
12	repeat 3 times
4	**lift* up into knee stand with *contraction* (Fig. 119.3) - 1 ct. *release*
4	lower into knee sit with *contraction* - 1 ct. *release*
8	repeat
	repeat whole sequence

119.1   *119.2*

119.3

4.4.3 Barre

EXERCISE 11: "FLAT BACK AND CONTRACTION"

Starting position: standing facing the barre, 2nd position parallel, hands hold the barre at shoulder width, torso and legs are at an angle of 90 degrees.

cts. Sequence	Fig. 120.1-3

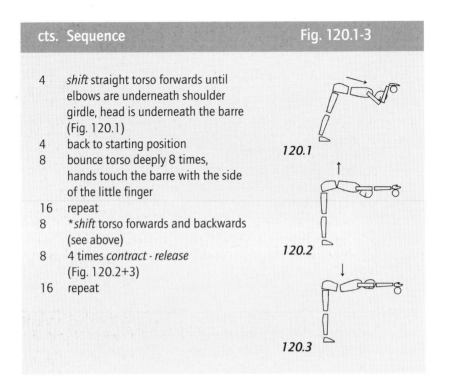

4	*shift* straight torso forwards until elbows are underneath shoulder girdle, head is underneath the barre (Fig. 120.1)	
4	back to starting position	
8	bounce torso deeply 8 times, hands touch the barre with the side of the little finger	
16	repeat	
8	**shift* torso forwards and backwards (see above)	
8	4 times *contract - release* (Fig. 120.2+3)	
16	repeat	

120.1

120.2

120.3

Mistakes

- Rounding the whole spine during the *contraction.*

How to correct

- Concentrate wholly on *contracting and releasing* the gluteals. Tactile help: put hands with only little pressure onto the lumbar vertebrae.

EXERCISE 12: "BOUNCING PLIÉS"

Sequence

Cf. Model Lesson 1, p. 55.

EXERCISE 13: "PLIÉS"

Starting position: standing facing the barre, 1st position turned out, both hands hold the barre (Fig. without barre).

cts. Sequence   Fig. 121.1+2

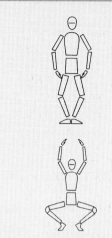

4	*demi plié* and stretch (Fig. 121.1)
4	repeat
8	**grand plié* and stretch (Fig. 121.2) change through closing the feet into 1st position parallel,
4	*demi plié* and stretch
4	repeat
8	**grand plié* and stretch
4	*demi plié* - stretch and pull up into *relevé*
4	change of position: *plié* - stretch and *turn* out *tendu* to the right side into 2nd position

cts. Sequence (continued)   Fig. 122.1-3

4	*demi plié* and stretch (Fig. 122.1)
4	repeat
8	**grand plié* and stretch (Fig. 122.2) change into 2nd position parallel
4	*demi plié* and stretch
4	repeat
8	**grand plié* and stretch
4	*demi plié* - stretch and *relevé*
4	lower and *plié, turn* out into 2nd position - stretch * BALANCE
4	rise slowly into the *relevé* position, *lift* arms sideways and then up into 3rd position (Fig.122.3)
4	hold position
4	lower heels
4	lower arms and neutral position

122.1

122.2

122.3

Mistakes
- Knees fall inwards when doing the *grand plié*.
- Bottom "sits on the heels".
- No continuity of control in the rhythmical-dynamic process resulting in a pause at the point of return.

How to correct
- Open the knee with outward pull backwards, place weight over all toes.
- Press pelvis forwards and upwards, without relaxing in between, the joints are bent consciously.
- See Model Lesson 1, Exercise 11.

EXERCISE 14: "PLIÉ RELEVÉ"

Starting position: 2nd position turned out, both hands hold the barre.

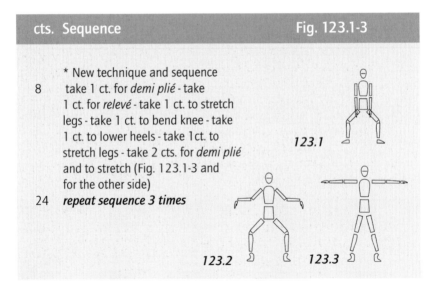

cts.	Sequence	Fig. 123.1-3
8	* New technique and sequence take 1 ct. for *demi plié* - take 1 ct. for *relevé* - take 1 ct. to stretch legs - take 1 ct. to bend knee - take 1 ct. to lower heels - take 1 ct. to stretch legs - take 2 cts. for *demi plié* and to stretch (Fig. 123.1-3 and for the other side)	123.1
24	*repeat sequence 3 times*	123.2 123.3

EXERCISE 15: "LEG STRETCHING IN LUNGE POSITION"

Starting position: standing facing the barre. Hands hold the barre, legs are parallel with the weight over the right leg, which is at the front, and on the balls of the left leg.

cts.	Sequence	Fig. 124.1-6

	* New technique and sequence	
6	bounce left heel to the ground 6 times, bend and stretch right knee simultaneously, leave left leg straight (Fig. 124.1)	
2	*change of positions:* bring left knee forwards and raise - put foot down next to right leg - raise right knee - put right foot down backwards onto ball (Fig. 124.2)	*124.1*
8	*repeat for the other side* *change of positions:* take hands off the barre, left foot slides out backwards into a deep *lunge* position, the right bent leg is turned out, hands support to the left and right of the knee (Fig.124.3)	*124.2*
8	8 bounces of the pelvis forwards-downwards with simultaneous pull of the left heel backwards	*124.3*
4	*change legs:* in deep *plié* put left foot next to right foot (Fig.124.4) - right foot slides out backwards until leg is straight	
12	repeat the bounces and the change of legs for the other side	*124.4*
4	4 bounces of the pelvis forwards-downwards with simultaneous pull of the left heel backwards	
8	stretch right leg and bring torso next to right leg, starting from the sternum, hold lengthening position (Fig. 124.5)	*124.5*
12	repeat	
4	*change legs*, see above	
8	take 4 cts. to run forwards on hands until torso is straight parallel to the floor - hold for 4 cts. (Fig. 124.6)	*124.6*
4	*change legs*, see above	
8	repeat for the other side	

Mistakes

- Weight of the body is not exactly placed between both legs in the lunge position.
- Pelvis is turned and raised towards the side of the rear leg.

How to correct

- The lower leg of the front leg should at least be vertical.
- Turn the pelvis parallel to the floor.

EXERCISE 16: STRETCHING; LEG ON BARRE

Starting position: standing facing the barre, legs are parallel, right foot rests on the barre with the knee bent, hands hold onto the barre next to foot, torso is upright (Fig. 125.1)

cts.	Sequence	Fig. 125.1+2
4	stretch right leg, rounded torso rests on leg	
4	bend right leg and starting position	
8	repeat	
4	stretch right leg, rounded torso rests on leg	
4	*take 2 cts. to pull torso forwards - take 2 cts. to stretch torso and to bend right leg (Fig. 125.2)	
24	repeat 3 times	
	repeat sequence with the other leg	

EXERCISE 17: "BEND AND BOUNCE"

Starting position: right side faces the barre, bent right leg is on the barre, arch rests on the barre, the right hand holds the barre in front of the right foot.

cts. Sequence	Fig. 126.1-3

*Fast changes of the torso position are new

8 bounce rounded torso deeply (Fig. 126.1)

8 bounce torso deeply with *flat back* (Fig. 126.2)

8 bounce rounded torso 4 times deeply and then with *flat back*

4 bounce rounded torso 2 times deeply and then with *flat back*

8 repeat 4 times alternating between rounded and *flat back*

8 *straighten up torso into neutral position, *turn* out supporting leg (which is taking over the weight), arms in 3rd position, *lift* up right leg and lower it again slowly
repeat sequence with the other leg

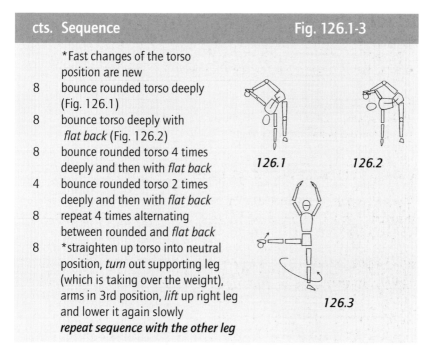

126.1   126.2

126.3

EXERCISE 18: "SIDE SPLIT"

Starting position: standing facing the barre on turned out right leg, left leg is on the barre, both hands hold the barre.

cts. Sequence	Fig. 127.1

*New technique and sequence

8 bring supporting leg into *plié* position and stretch (Fig. 127.1)

8 bring supporting leg into *relevé* position and lower it again

4 bend torso to the left, right arm in 3rd position

4 straighten torso up and change arms

4 bend torso to the right, left arm in 3rd position

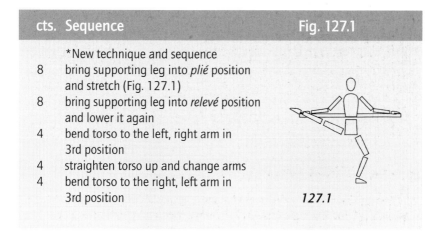

127.1

cts.	Sequence	Fig. 127.2+3

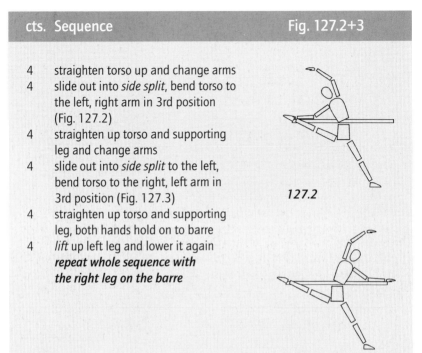

cts.	Sequence
4	straighten torso up and change arms
4	slide out into *side split*, bend torso to the left, right arm in 3rd position (Fig. 127.2)
4	straighten up torso and supporting leg and change arms
4	slide out into *side split* to the left, bend torso to the right, left arm in 3rd position (Fig. 127.3)
4	straighten up torso and supporting leg, both hands hold on to barre
4	*lift* up left leg and lower it again **repeat whole sequence with the right leg on the barre**

127.2

127.3

Mistakes

• Torso is not bent sideways in the frontal plane.
• Foot of the supporting leg falls onto the instep in order to expand the slide into the *split*.
• Hip of the supporting leg or the torso move sideways when the leg is *lifted* up.

How to correct

• See correction Exercise 14.
• Keep the weight over the outer edge of the foot, do not stretch over the limit.
• See Model Lesson 1, Exercise 15.

EXERCISE 19: "LEG FORTIFICATION"

Starting position: standing facing the barre in 2nd position turned out, hands hold the barre.

cts. Sequence	Fig. 128.1-3

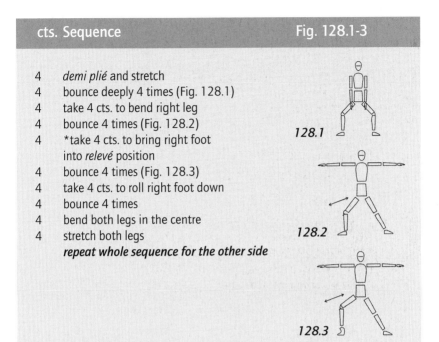

4	*demi plié* and stretch
4	bounce deeply 4 times (Fig. 128.1)
4	take 4 cts. to bend right leg
4	bounce 4 times (Fig. 128.2)
4	*take 4 cts. to bring right foot
	into *relevé* position
4	bounce 4 times (Fig. 128.3)
4	take 4 cts. to roll right foot down
4	bounce 4 times
4	bend both legs in the centre
4	stretch both legs

repeat whole sequence for the other side

128.1

128.2

128.3

EXERCISE 20: "LEG SWINGS"

Sequence
Cf. Model Lesson 1, p. 138.

4.4.4 Floor Work 2

EXERCISE 21: "ROLL UP AND DOWN"

Sequence
Cf. Model Lesson 1, p. 140, *tempo-variation:* the whole sequence is now repeated over 2 cts. for each stage.

EXERCISE 22: "LEG WORK BACK"

Sequence
Cf. Model Lesson 1, p. 141.

EXERCISE 23: "BATTEMENTS"

Starting position: lying on the back with support of the forearms*.

cts.	Sequence	Fig. 129.1+2

PART 1*

4	bend right leg and stretch up vertically (Fig. 129.1+2)	
8	*flex and point* right foot 4 times	
4	lower right leg	
8	4 straight *battements* forwards and upwards	
32	repeat sequence with left leg	

For **PART 2** see Model Lesson 1, p. 92.

cts.	Sequence (continued)	Fig. 130.1-4

PART 3*

starting position: lying on the right side, legs *turned* out, head rests on the straight right arm, left arm supports in front of the body

2	right leg *passé* and stretch vertically (Fig. 130.1)	*130.1*
2	lower the leg with *flexed* foot	
4	repeat	
16	8 straight *battements* sideways (Fig. 130.2)	
2	4 fast small *battements* with *flexed* foot, emphasize the closing phase (Fig. 130.3)	*130.2*
2	1 high *battement* with *pointed-flexed* foot	
4	repeat	*130.3*
8	raise legs and upper body and *balance* on the right side, arms in 3rd position (Fig. 130.4)	
4	roll over the back onto the left side *repeat whole sequence with the left leg*	*130.4*

Mistakes
- Part 1: shoulder girdle is pushed up.
- Parts 2+3: pelvis is tilted backwards when lying on the side, tensed shoulders.

How to correct
- Make the spine long and pull shoulders down.
- See Model Lesson 1, Exercise 18.

4.4.5 Isolation

The *isolation technique* is practised further on in the same sequence as suggested by BERNARD, as described in *Model Lesson 1, Section 4.3.5*. The exercises can be executed and given a rhythm with a faster tempo. For examples of polycentric coordination exercises see Section 5.

EXERCISE 24: "HEAD ISOLATION" (CF. P. 144)

EXERCISE 25: "SHOULDER ISOLATION" (CF. P. 145)

EXERCISE 26: "CHEST ISOLATION" (CF. P. 145)

EXERCISE 27: "PELVIS ISOLATION" (CF. P. 146)

EXERCISE 28: "HAND ISOLATION" (CF. P. 147)

EXERCISE 29: "BRUSHES"

Starting position: 1st position parallel, arms in neutral position.

cts.	Sequence	Fig. 131.1-3

For **PART 1** see Model Lesson 1,
p. 147 (Fig. 131.1+2)
PART 2*

4	*plié - turn* legs out in 1st position - stretch legs - brush foot out sideways on the right
8	8 *brushes* to the right, the emphasis is on pulling the foot back towards the body
8	8 *brushes* to the left side
4	4 *brushes* to the right side
4	4 *brushes* to the left side
2	2 *brushes* to the left side
2	2 *brushes* to the right side
8	8 *brushes* to the right side and to the left side alternately
4	finish the sequence with a *plié*

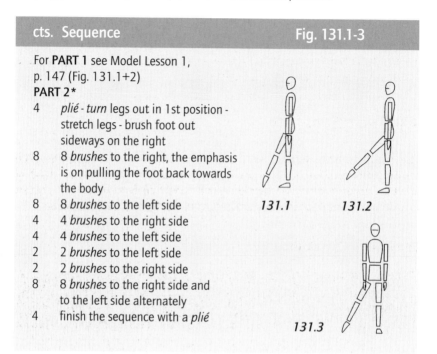

131.1   *131.2*

131.3

EXERCISE 30: "JUMPS"

Starting position: 1st position turned out, arms in neutral position.

cts.	Sequence

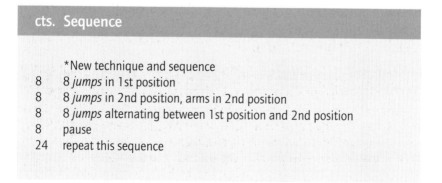

	*New technique and sequence
8	8 *jumps* in 1st position
8	8 *jumps* in 2nd position, arms in 2nd position
8	8 *jumps* alternating between 1st position and 2nd position
8	pause
24	repeat this sequence

Mistakes
* Foot and knee joints are not completely straight in the flying phase.
* Pelvis is moved backwards in the landing phase, heels do not completely touch the floor.

How to correct
* The techniques for the *demi plié* and *relevé* positions are now required and must constantly be practised in preparation.

4.4.6 Across the Floor

The *Jazz Walks* from **Model Lesson 1** are practised further on and they are linked in new combinations as suggested in the *catalogue of exercises, section 3.4.8*. In addition, depending on the grade of their groups, trainers can offer the dancers an unlimited number of new steps, rhythms and combinations of movements.

EXERCISE 31: "STEP-TIP"

Variation 1 (cf. Model Lesson 1, p. 111)	
Variation 2	
2	*step* to the right - *tip* with the left foot
2	*step* to the left - *tip* with the right foot
4	on 1st ct. *step* forwards with the right foot - on 2nd ct. *step* backwards with the left foot - 3rd ct. pause - 4th ct. (and 4): *step* backwards on the right foot, put weight briefly over the balls of the feet - *step* forwards on the left foot (*ball change*)

EXERCISE 32: "CONTRACTION WALK"

Variation	
1	put right foot forwards with *contract-release*
1	put the whole weight over right foot with *contract-release*
1	put left foot forwards with *contract-release*
1	put the whole weight over right foot with *contract-release*

EXERCISE 33: "SIDE WALK + LEG ROTATION"

Variation 1: Side to Side

8	4 *side walks with leg rotation* to the right, with the last step bring the left foot next to the body on the balls of the feet, without putting any weight over the balls of the feet
8	4 *side walks with leg rotation* to the left
4	repeat 2 *side walks* to the right
4	repeat 2 *side walks* to the left
4	*side walk* alternately to the right and to the left

Variation 2: Arm Coordination

Starting position: arms in 1st *jazz position*, finger tips touch the sternum

2	*side walk* to the right, *right arm:* open to the side - close
2	*side walk* to the right, *right arm:* open to the front - close
2	*side walk* to the right, *left arm:* open to the side - close
2	*side walk* to the right, *left arm:* open to the front - close
8	*repeat sequence for the other side*

EXERCISE 34: "SIDE WALK + HIP SHIFT"

Variation: Contract-Release

2	*side walk* to the right with hip *shift* to the left - simultaneously 2 times *contract-release* with the right side
	repeat continuously or side to side with changes of direction

EXERCISE 35: "STEP-TIP + SIDE WALK-LEG ROTATION"

Combination

4	2 times *step-tip* forwards, starting on the right foot
4	2 *side walks* to the right: open - close - open - close with a *tip* of the left foot without putting any weight over that foot
8	repeat, starting with the left foot
	repeat continuously alternating between right foot and left foot

EXERCISE 36: "CONTRACTION WALK + SIDE WALK - HIP LIFT"

Combination

4	*contraction walk* on the right and on the left foot forwards
4	*4 contraction walks* (at double speed)
8	*4 side walks* with *hip lift* to the right, bring foot next to body on last step, without putting any weight over it
16	repeat, starting on the left foot
	repeat continuously alternating between right foot and left foot

EXERCISE 37: "STEP-TIP-BALL CHANGE + SIDE WALK-ARM COORDINATION"

Combination

4	2 times *step-tip* forwards, starting on the right foot
4	on 1st ct.: *step* forwards on the right foot - 2nd ct.: *step* backwards on the left foot - 3rd ct.: pause - 4th ct. (and 4): *step* backwards on the right foot, put weight briefly over the balls of the feet and *step* forwards on the left foot
8	*see Exercise 32, variation 2*

EXERCISE 38: "SWINGS"

Sequence
Cf. Model Lesson 1, p. 151.

5 SEQUENCES OF EXERCISES FOR THE SYSTEMATIC DEVELOPMENT OF INDIVIDUAL JAZZ DANCE TECHNIQUES

Based on the author's experience in the areas of training sports teachers and of working with amateur dancers, sequences of exercises are described in the following chapter with which individual dance techniques like *pliés, falls, turns and jumps* can be developed.

They are independent of the model lessons of ALAIN BERNARD even if there may be similarities in the structure of a lesson and even if individual sequences of exercises are applied.

Methodical Conception

A choice of 6 techniques was made. 5 of the techniques: *pliés, jazz split, contraction fall, back fall, hop and side fall* are developed with sequences of exercises which build on one another in the following steps:

Step 1:

Floor Work with preparatory exercises which concentrate on the **development of technical-coordinative and conditional requirements**. *Floor Work* in various lying levels, sitting levels and knee stands provides useful feedback on posture and tension of the muscles, excludes balance problems, builds a good basis for the development of mobility and torso strength and enables the dancers to learn **certain parts** of the individual technique consciously. To facilitate a high level of concentration and to give the dancers a chance to make their own experiences, it is best to present the movements purely verbally without demonstrating them and to accompany them with rhythms.

Step 2:

To **develop more complex aspects** of the technique and to make the conditions a bit more difficult, sequences of exercises at **the barre** are then executed, with the barre primarily used to help the dancers to maintain balance but also contributing to the further development of strength and mobility. The ability to coordinate more complex movements executed with the whole body is trained increasingly. This is the point to introduce music during the lessons, suggestions for music were made in Model Lesson 1.

Step 3:

This step includes further development of the technique in question, of possibilities to vary and combine it (successively and simultaneously) in free space, in standing, over several spatial planes (Centre Work) and in locomotion (Across the Floor). In this step the forms are developed which, in combination with other techniques, are required for artistic dance designs.

There is no Floor Work in preparation for the **turns.** Although working at the barre is an important requirement for turns on one leg and has been described in the catalogue of exercises, it is not relevant here since more simple turns are presented in the following sections. The individual steps are mostly

1. preparatory stage and take off phase
2. turning phase with gradually increased turning degree
3. combining the turning directions right and left.

As an appendix to the sequences of exercises a few combinations of exercises involving the technique of **"Polycentrics"** in standing and in locomotion have been added from the author's work experience. Particular isolated mobility in all body centres (cf. section 3.2) is a requirement and can be prepared through the exercises for isolation technique (see catalogue of exercises and model lessons).

Specifications on How to Apply the Sequences of Exercises in the Lessons

Teachers or trainers will decide, according to their topic, the needs of their group or the requirements of a curriculum, when and at which point in a sequence of lessons or within a training period it makes sense to incorporate such sequences of exercises. The decision about how much time to take for the individual stages of movement should also be taken by the teachers or should be made on the basis of the model lessons in section 4 to guarantee as much flexibility as possible. The hints as to how often an individual exercise should be repeated should thus be taken as recommendations. If sequences of exercises of individual techniques on the floor or at the barre coincide, no detailed description is given for them.

In the following descriptions, references will be made constantly to hints about terms, technical characteristics, functions of exercises, mistakes and how to correct them, examples of music and illustrations in the catalogue of exercises and in the model lessons given earlier in this book.

5.1 Pliés

This dance technique is developed here through exercises in various positions on the floor and subsequently at the barre. The final step is the free standing position, which should only be introduced after a considerable period of training so that no incorrect strain can occur. It is useful for the dancers' concentration and for the correction work to accompany the floor work purely verbally and to introduce slow, continuous music only when working at the barre (for examples of music, see **Model Lesson 1**).

No detailed descriptions of exercises which have already been covered in the catalogue or in the model lessons will be given. (For technical and functional hints on *pliés*, see catalogue of exercises.)

5.1.1 Floor Work

Sequence of exercises 1 "Pliés"   Notes on procedure

"*Pliés* in 1st position lying on the back"
Starting position: lying on the back, feet are flat on the floor at width of hips, arms in 2nd position.

1. *Flex* right foot - bring heel towards the left knee and open angle of knee (to about 135 degrees), until the sole of the foot points parallel towards the ceiling (*table top* position).
- Stretch joint of the foot and toes successively - *flex* joint of the foot and toes successively.

Repeat 3 times
- Stretch right leg and right foot towards the ceiling - bend foot and knee into *demi plié* and stretch again

Repeat 3 times
- Right leg *plié* - lower leg and place heel next to supporting leg - roll sole of foot down.

Slow and conscious execution with self-monitoring, foot and knee must be in the perpendicular throughout.

During the *plié* the thigh bends towards the chest, the sole of the foot is parallel to the ceiling, use the foot joints and the phalanges consciously. Execute the stretching phase of the leg with the visualisation "Press against the ceiling".

2. Repeat sequence with the left leg.
3. Repeat sequence with the right leg and the left leg *outwardly rotated.*
4. Repeat sequence of exercise with both legs *outwardly rotated.*

The *outward rotation* starts from the hip joint. Check that the heel and the hip joint remain in one single line during the *plié* and that the foot achieves *table top* position.

"Pliés in 2nd position lying on the side"
Starting position: lying on the left side, legs closed outwardly rotated, head rests on extended left arm, right arm supports in front of the chest.

1. Right leg *passé* and stretch towards the ceiling - *flex* foot and stretch it.
Repeat 3 times
- Bend right leg into *demi plié* and stretch towards the ceiling again - repeat several times.
- Lower straight right leg - body roll over the back into lying on the right side.
2. Repeat sequence with the left leg.

The body makes a single line from head to toe, do not move forwards or backwards in the pelvis, free leg remains in outward rotation (starting from the hip joint) throughout, during *plié* knee and foot are in the perpendicular, foot in *table top* position.

Sequence of exercises 2 "Pliés"

Notes on procedure

"Pliés in 1st sitting position.
Starting position: sitting with closed straight legs parallel, upright posture, hands support on the fingertips at the back.

Help: partner supports pelvis and back or sitting against the wall.

1. *Flex* and stretch feet.
Repeat 3 times
- Legs into *demi plié* and stretch.
Repeat 3 times
2. Bend legs into *grand plié* - stretch feet in this position up to the maximal point and roll down again into *flex position.*
Repeat 3 times

Heels stay on their point of contact and are only rolled over. Good upright posture, check the perpendicular position of knee and foot posture.

Maximal bend of the leg with upright pelvis, knee and feet in one single line.

3. Repeat exercise 1 with **outward rotation** of the legs.
4. Repeat exercise 2 with **outward rotation** of the legs.

In the outward rotation only the outer edge of the foot respectively the side of the little toe is in contact with the floor.

"*Pliés* in 2nd sitting position"
Starting position: sitting with open straight legs parallel, upright posture, hands support on the fingertips at the back.

1. See Model Lessons 1+2, section: Floor Work 1, exercise: "Pliés" (p. 163).
2. Roll right leg in - *demi plié* - roll leg out - stretch.
- Roll left leg in - *demi plié* - roll leg out - stretch.
  Roll both legs in - *demi plié* - roll legs out - stretch.
Repeat 3 times
3. Repeat exercise 2 reversed: roll out - *demi plié* - roll in - stretch.

Slow execution of the movement at first with **partner's help** and self-control, then with arm and head coordination.

Ensure good upright posture, which is reinforced by inhalation during the *plié*, and perpendicular posture of the joints.

5.1.2 Barre

Sequence of exercises 3 "Pliés"

Notes on procedure

Sequence of exercises 3 "Pliés"	Notes on procedure
"Bouncing *Pliés*" "*Pliés*" "*Plié-Relevé*" *See Model Lesson 1+2, section: Barre*	Slow and continuous execution of the movements, correction via the mirror and the teacher. Higher level of difficulty. Standing sideways to the barre, one hand holds the barre.

5.1.3 Centre Work

Sequence of exercises 4 "Pliés" Notes on procedure

"Demi and *Grand Pliés"*
Starting position: 1st position parallel, arms straight in 2nd position, hands face forwards.

1. 2 times *demi plié* and stretch the legs - *grand plié* and stretch, arm coordination: straight forwards - bend - forwards - open to the sides - *demi plié*, lower arms - stretch legs and *relevé, lift* arms forwards then up into 3rd position - lower the heels.
Repeat exercise 1 time

Slow and continuous execution with regular breathing. For criteria for the technique see catalogue of exercises (p. 55)

2. Repeat exercise 2 times in *1st position outwardly rotated.*
3. Repeat exercise 2 times in *2nd position parallel.*
4. Repeat exercise 2 times in *2nd position outwardly rotated.*

Immediate change of position through outward rotation of the legs and the toe tips (pull the buttocks together).
Immediate change of position through opening the heels. Do not exceed width of hips!
Open to outward rotation, see above, expand position over width of hips.

"Plié - Relevé"
Starting position: 1st position parallel, arms in 2nd *jazz position.*

1. *Demi plié - lift* heels *(relevé)* - stretch legs - lower heels.
Repeat 3 times.
2. *Relevé* - bend knees - lower heels *(demi plié)* - stretch legs.
Repeat 3 times.
3. Repeat exercises 1+2 in outwardly rotated 1st position.

For change of positions see above. In the *plié - relevé* positions *shift* the knees exactly over the toes over which the weight is equally distributed. Do not move backwards with the pelvis.

4. Repeat exercises 1+2 in 2nd position parallel and in outwardly rotated 2nd position.

Plié - relevé
Starting position: 2nd position parallel.

1. Raise right heel and *turn* leg in - both legs *demi plié*, right heel remains raised - *turn* leg parallel - lower the heel.
2. Repeat, starting with the left leg.
Repeat 3 times for the right leg and for the left leg.

Rotate only the leg in and out, starting from the hip joint, the body remains in the frontal plane, the knee is always in the perpendicular position with the foot.

5.2 Jazz Split

The first sequence of exercises should be preceded by general warm-up and flexibility exercises like for example from the section *Floor Work 1*: "FLEXIBILITY OF FEET AND LEGS" (p. 49) or "BEND AND BOUNCES" (p. 37).

(For technical and functional hints and illustrations on *jazz splits* see catalogue of exercises, p. 82).

5.2.1 Floor Work

Sequence of exercises 1 "Jazz Split"   Notes on procedure

"Leg Stretching while lying on the back and on the stomach"
Starting position: lying on the back, legs straight and closed, arms next to the body.

1. Bend right leg and hold with both hands under the thigh - stretch leg towards the ceiling and hold.
- Flex foot 4 times and stretch.

Back and pelvis remain on the floor, pull the shoulder down consciously and do not tense neck muscles. You may want to use "relaxing music".

- Pull leg closer towards the body with the hands and hold.
- *Lift* left arm on the floor upwards and roll slowly over onto the stomach, the right hand remains around the right leg which is still pulled towards the body.
- Put forehead onto the left hand and hold lengthening position.
- Roll back onto back, put both hands around leg and pull it towards the body - lower straight leg.
2. Repeat sequence of exercises with the left leg.

Start rotation from the pelvis, turn leg outwards extensively, do not *"fall"* onto the stomach, use support of the left arm.

Execute this extreme lengthening position only after a warm-up phase. When lying on the stomach try to bring the body from head to foot of "supporting" leg into one single axis and to bring the pelvis towards the floor through relaxation, using exhalation consciously.

"Hip Stretching"
Starting position: sitting in 4th position (swastika).
For sequence of exercises see *catalogue of exercises, Floor Work 2, p. 94.*

"Leg Work Back"
Starting position: lying on the stomach, head rests on the hands.
For sequence of exercises see *catalogue of exercises, Floor Work 2, p. 86.*

"Attitude +Jazz Split"
Starting position: lying on the stomach, arms in 2nd position.

Development of an *attitude* position back: the knee points towards the ceiling, the groin is straight, arms and upper body remain on the floor.

1. Raise bent right leg - cross backwards over the left leg, toe *tip* touches the floor (attitude) - stretch right leg again lying on the stomach and lower leg.
Repeat with left leg.
2. Cross right leg backwards (see above) - place onto floor with rotation to the right side - support pelvis upwards with left hand, right foot stands on the ball - slide out into *jazz split* left diagonally forwards.

In the *jazz split* large angle in the backward leg (*attitude*), hip is straight, knee should not touch the floor.

- Pull left leg back towards the vertical line of the body and roll over the right side onto the stomach.
Repeat with left leg.
Repeat whole sequence several times.

5.2.2 Barre

Sequence of exercises 2 "Jazz Split"   Notes on procedure

"Side and Forward"
Starting position: facing the barre, side of the right leg rests on the barre, both legs turned out, hands hold the barre.

1. Slide out to the right side into *split* - pull back into centre.

Very calm execution with music, hold lengthening position in *split*, legs *turned* out, whole torso turned exactly into the respective front.

- Turn left side towards the barre, right arm in 3rd position.
2. Slide out frontally into *split* - pull back into the centre.
3. Repeat the *split* bending the torso forwards.
- Pull back towards the centre and straighten up torso.

4. Repeat *split* with both arms in 3rd position - straighten up and *turn* front towards the barre.

- *Relevé* and lower, arms in 3rd position, raise right leg, lower arms and leg.
Repeat whole sequence with left leg on the barre.

Raise and lower leg slowly, torso remains in perpendicular position (do not tilt sideways).

5.2.3 Centre Work

Sequence of exercises 3 "Jazz Split"   Notes on procedure

"Jazz Split from Standing Position"
Starting position: standing, 1st or 5th position.

1. Press upwards from the left foot into *plié-relevé* position - right leg slides out diagonally to the right side forwards - the right arm supports at the back near the body centre of gravity - slide out with straight right leg, straight left groin and bent left leg into *jazz split* onto the floor.
2. Find form of standing up or see catalogue of exercises p. 84.
Repeat for the other side.

The body centre of gravity should be between both legs when sliding out and the rear leg should remain in a good outwardly rotated position, to prevent the knee from falling onto the floor. Various forms of standing up can be tried out in order to subsequently practise the *jazz split* left.

"Jazz Split from Locomotion"
1. 4 *steps* starting on the right foot - slide out into *jazz split* to the right side - for standing up see above.
- Repeat, starting on the right leg.
Repeat sequence continuously changing between right leg and left leg.

One sequence of movement (right) over 12 cts. Variation: 2 *steps* - 1 *chassé* forwards and slide out into *split*.

5.3 Contraction Fall

In the following sequences the floor work serves to build up the necessary strength in the abdominals, the buttocks and the thigh muscles and also the development of the *contraction*. Balance support through the barre helps to get from a standing position with *table top* position of the torso into the *contraction plié* position. A lot of strength and balance is required to be able to rapidly build up shoulder, hip and foot joints vertically one above the other and then to lower the body centre of gravity in this position (feet in *relevé* position).

Only when these positions can be executed smoothly is it possible to roll down from the *contraction plié* position without touching the floor with the knees.
(For technical and functional hints and illustrations see *catalogue of exercises, p. 82, p. 102*).

5.3.1 Floor Work

Sequence of exercises 1a "Contraction Fall"   Notes on procedure

"Strengthening of the Abdominals and the Buttocks"
Starting position: lying on the back, feet are flat on the floor, arms in 2nd position.

1. Raise the coccyx and roll the pelvis up to the thoracic vertebrae, groins are straight, buttocks are tensed - hold position and roll down slowly. *Repeat 3 times.*

Breathe constantly. Do not "press" stomach but let it "fall" towards the spine. Waist remains fixed on the floor, the buttocks are tensed and "pull the groins long".

2. Roll head and torso up to the waist, arms extended forwards - hold position and roll down again slowly. *Repeat 3 times.*

Do not pull shoulders up, carry head freely, exhale continuously.

3. Remain in rolled up position and make 8-16 small bounces with the torso forwards
Repeat 2 times

"Contraction in Knee Stand"
Starting position: knee stand with support on the forearms.

1. *Contract* abdominals and gluteals until lumbar vertebrae are rounded - release.
Repeat 7 times.

Slow execution, mind continuous breathing, work only in the pelvis and in the area of the lumbar vertebrae.

Starting position: knee sit, arms extended forwards, hands holding ankles.

2. *See catalogue of exercises, Floor Work 1, p. 49/50.*

For tips on how to execute these see *catalogue of exercises and Model Lesson 1.*

"Swinging"
Starting position: squat, open at hip width, hands support at the back, fingers point forwards.

1. *Lift* pelvis up at the back between the arms - *swing* pelvis forwards with *contraction* and *shift* the open knees far over the feet, feet in *relevé* position - *swing* pelvis back between the arms.
Repeat 7 times.

Abdominals and buttocks remain *contract*ed throughout, tilt the pelvis backwards like a "cup". Warning: no lordosis! With the groins completely straight, the forward thigh muscles are lengthened.

5.3.2 Barre

Sequence of exercises 2 "Contraction Fall"

"Contraction Fall and Jazz Split"
Starting position: right side faces the barre, standing parallel at width of hips, left arm in 3rd position, right hand holds the barre.

For sequence of exercise see *catalogue of exercises, 3.5.4 Barre*, "Contraction Fall and Jazz Split", *Part 1*.

See *catalogue of exercises*

5.3.3 Centre Work

Sequence of exercises 3 "Contraction Fall"   Notes on procedure

"Contraction Pliés"
1. *Contraction* with *demi plié* - make *plié* deeper, heels raise from the floor, arms are *shifted* forwards with pressure - straighten up body with pressure into *relevé* position - lower heels and arms slowly.
Repeat 3 times.

The movement starts with the *contraction*, shoulder girdle and pelvic girdle remain in perpendicular position throughout. With enough practice the *plié* can be deepened until the knees almost reach the floor.

"Contraction Fall"
Starting position: 2nd position parallel, arms in 2nd position.

2. Lower torso with *flat back - demi plié - contraction plié* (see above) - tilt torso forwards into *flat back* position with straight legs - straighten up torso.
3. Repeat up to *contraction plié* - deepen until the knees are just above the floor - roll over onto the stomach over the right side, lower with legs bent - roll on into sitting position and stand up over one leg.
Repeat for the other side.

Roll onto the stomach with straight groins, hands support the torso.

5.4 Back Fall

The *back fall* can be developed from grade 3 onwards. A requirement for the execution of this *fall* is the floor- and barre work for the *contraction fall* (p. 82-84).

Here the *contraction pliés* with *twist* and the development of the *falling* phase backwards with support of a partner are new. (For technical and functional notes and illustrations see **catalogue of exercises, p. 103/104**).

5.4.1 Floor Work

See sequence of exercises 1 for *contraction fall*, p. 186.

5.4.2 Barre

See sequence of exercises 2 for *contraction fall*, p. 187.

5.4.3 Centre Work

Sequence of exercises 3

Notes on procedure

Contraction "Plié +Twist"
Starting position: 2nd position parallel, arms in 2nd *jazz position*.

1. - *Contraction* with *demi plié*, deepen the *plié* and twist the upper body to the right side simultaneously, move arms parallel to the twisted shoulder girdle from downwards forwards and then backwards.
- straighten up and *turn* forwards with *relevé* - lower the heels and the arms.
2. Repeat the movement for the other side.
Repeat 3 times.

Bend the knees over the feet, do not tilt towards the twisted side. Ensure that pelvis remains in frontal plane.

"Back Fall"
Starting position: 2nd position parallel, right arm in neutral position, left hand holds partner.

1. *Contraction plié* - deepen until knee is just above the floor - twist upper body to the right side, right arm makes circle backwards - lower torso backwards to the right side until right shoulder touches the floor - slide out onto the back.
Repeat for the other side.
2. Without help of a partner starting from various positions.

Partner provides counterweight to prevent "*falling*" onto the shoulder.

Only when the dancer has developed the technique and enough strength can the *back fall* be executed without help.

5.5 Hop and Side Fall

In the following sequences of exercises first the basic technical training of the starting and the landing phases for the *jump* is prepared and then more specifically the *hop* with *passé*. The technique of the *side fall* is first developed slowly in the standing position and then linked in locomotion with *steps* and the *hop*.

To develop general technical-coordinative and conditional requirements the "*pliés* on the floor" (sequence of exercises 1+2) should precede this sequence of exercises.

(For technical and functional notes and illustrations *see catalogue of exercises*.)

5.5.1 Centre Work

Sequence of exercises 1
"Hop and Side Fall"   Notes on procedure "Plié-Relevé"

Starting position: 1st position parallel, arms in 2nd *jazz position*.

1. *Demi plié - relevé* - stretch knees - lower heels.
   - *Relevé* - bend knees - lower heels - stretch knees.
2. *grand plié*, close arm for 1st *jazz position* - stretch legs, open arms for 2nd *jazz position - relevé*, raise arms for 3rd *jazz position* - lower heels - lower arms into 2nd jazz position.
Repeat exercises 1+2 3 times.

"Foot and Leg Work"
Starting position: see above, arms in neutral position.

Torso in good upright position, slow execution of movement with music.

1. Roll right heel up until standing on the ball - stretch toes and lengthen excessively - roll down toes again until standing on the ball - roll foot down onto the heel.
- Repeat with left foot.
Repeat exercise 3 times.
2. Same exercise as above but now the heel and the toes bound off the floor one after the other. Rolling up, however, is slow with pressure into the floor.
3. Same exercise as above but now the whole foot bounds off the floor in one single movement ("take off". For rolling down see above.
4. Same exercise as above starting from the *demi plié* position, stretch supporting leg when "taking off" on the foot of the free leg.
- When rolling down the foot go back into *demi plié* position.

Rolling the foot up, first slowly in separate phases then fast and vigorously in connected phases, corresponds with the foot work necessary to take off for a *jump, rolling the foot down* from the toes to the heel with pressure into the floor and then with *plié,* prepares for an elastic landing.

It is better to provide purely verbal accompaniment to this intensive and dynamically varied work.

Sequence of exercises 2 "Hop + Side Fall"

Notes on procedure "Foot and Jump Bounces"

Starting position: 1st position parallel, arms in 2nd position.

1. Lift into *relevé* and do 16 fast bounces on both legs in the foot joint with bent knees (foot bounce) - lower the heels - 2 *demi pliés* and stretch.
Repeat exercise 13 times.
2. 16 bounces with *demi plié* and with full stretch of the foot and knee joints (jump bounce).

Ensure good tension of the torso. Have pauses and do relaxation exercises after great strain through repetitions. Percussions and words accompany rhythmically.

"Passé"
Starting position: 1st position parallel, arms in neutral position.

1. Bound right foot off the floor 8 times and raise leg up to *passé* parallel position - roll foot down.
- Repeat 8 times with left leg.
2. Repeat 4 times with right and left leg.
3. Repeat 2 times with right and left leg.
4. Repeat alternately 8 times with right and left leg.

Ensure that the weight is only over the respective supporting leg, fix the hips by tensing the abductors: "pull the hip of the supporting leg inside".

"Passé and Side Fall"
Starting position: 1st position parallel, arms in neutral position.

- Right leg in *passé* parallel position, both arms in 3rd position - bend supporting leg down to squat, instep of the free leg touches the floor next to the supporting leg, hands support under the shoulder girdle.
- Slide out onto lying on the right side with support until the whole body is straight, the right arm lies in one line with the body on the floor under the arm, the left hand supports in front of the sternum.
- Straighten up into right knee stand, the left foot is flat on the floor - straighten up into standing position.

Repeat for the other side.

The knee of the free leg must not touch the floor, the weight is caught with the instep. Execute this movement very slowly and with control in its individual phases until the technical execution can be carried out smoothly. Then develop a fast, fall-like movement.

5.5.2 Across the Floor

Exercise 5 "Hop + Side Fall"

Notes on procedure
"Combination of Step, Hop
and Side Fall"

Starting position: standing on the left foot, right foot next to supporting leg with no weight over it, arms in neutral position.

1. 3 steps forwards - on 4th ct. left leg *passé* - 3 steps forwards (starting on the left foot) - on 4th ct. right leg *passé*. *Repeat continuously.*

The sequence of a combination on the right and on the left leg comprises 8 cts.

2. See above, on 3rd *step* with the right foot *demi plié*, on 4th ct. *relevé* on the right foot with *passé* of the left foot.
Repeat for the other side and continuously.

3. See above, on 3rd step bound off into *hop* with *passé* - on 4th ct. land on the same foot.
Repeat for the other side and continuously.

4. See above, land in squat, instep of the free leg on the floor - straighten up into standing position, take 8 cts. for whole sequence.
Repeat for the other side and continuously.

The Sequence of the combination right and left takes 16 cts.

5. See above, slide out from squat into sidefall, take 8 cts. for whole sequence.
- Take 4 cts. to straighten up into standing position.
Repeat for the other side and continuously.

The sequence of a combination to the right side and to the left side as described next to this is executed over 24 cts., but its time structure can be changed if necessary, e.g. to adapt to a piece of music.

5.6 Turns

General criteria for dance turns have already been described in the section *"Balance and Turns"*. For technical notes on ballet turns see the *catalogue of exercises* of ALAIN BERNARD.

The following sequences of exercises describe examples of various forms of turns taken from the author's experience of working with amateurs. Here again the main focus is on practising the preparatory positions (*préparations*), the *rotatory start*, the landing phase, support work of the arms and head control. Only the individual exercises which build on each other are described here; the technical progress of the group will determine how often each phase must be repeated.

5.6.1 Pivot Turn

The *pivot turn* consists of two steps. After a step forwards, which can also be executed as a *jazz lunge*, a quarter *turn* or half a *turn* (to the outside) follows in the direction of the leg with no weight over it and which is subsequently put under weight in the same place. This *step turn* is relatively easy, does not demand too much balance, and therefore serves to develop spatial orientation at beginner levels.

Grade 1

Sequence of exercises "Pivot Turn"   Notes on procedure

Starting position: these turns are practised as an extension to steps which here always start on the right foot.

1. 4 steps forwards - *jazz lunge* forwards on the right side, slightly rotated inwards, right hip visibly turned forwards, left arm forwards, right arm at the side - *shift* the weight back onto the left leg with a quarter *turn* to the left side.
Repeat continuously, then for the other side.

The result of this is a square which ensues after 6 steps, front and eyes also *turn* exactly in the new direction.

2. See above, after 4 steps forwards do a *pivot turn* with half a *turn*, then repeat the sequence in the opposite direction.

3. See above, after 4 steps forwards do two *pivot turns* one after the other. *Repeat sequence continuously in the same direction.*

Two *pivot turns* consist of two half *turns*. Make sure to spot the new direction in space after the half *turn*.

5.6.2 Turn Closed Parallel and Turned out

This *turn* (name by the author) is done on both feet. After pulling the feet rapidly together and up into a closed *relevé* position, the *turn* can be done to either side and it can have various degrees. Which leg starts the new movement after the *turn* is decided by the dancer or depends on the choice of the step combination to follow.

Grade 2

Sequence of exercises "Turn Closed"   Notes on procedure

Starting position: 1st position parallel, arms in 1st *jazz position.*
PHASE 1
1. Open right leg for 2nd position with *demi plié,* open arms for 2nd *jazz position (préparation).*
- Pull left leg next to right leg rapidly (close) stretching of both legs in *relevé* position, close arms for 1st *jazz position* - lower the heels.
Repeat for the other side.

During the *préparation* (here 2nd position *plié*) the weight should be put evenly over both feet, from which the take off follows, the arms help to "close" the whole body.

PHASES 2+3
2. *Préparation* to the right side (see above) - close with a quarter *turn* to the right side - préparation to the left side - close with a quarter *turn* to the left side.
Repeat for the other side.

The result of these steps is a square, with the *préparation* alternating between the right and the left side while the *turn* is always executed to the right side. It is very important to spot exactly in the new direction.

3. *Préparation* right - close with *half a turn to the right side.*
- Repeat and subsequently repeat for the other side.
4. *Préparation* right - close with a *full turn to the right side.*
- Repeat and subsequently repeat for the other side.
5. *Préparation* right - close with a *full turn to the left side.*
- Repeat and subsequently repeat for the other side.

Practise each exercise in this sequence in outwardly rotated position.

Subsequently the square is practised with continuous turning to the left side. In the half *turns* as in the quarter *turns*, the eyes spot exactly in the new direction, in the full *turn* the head must first be fixed in the starting direction and then, "overtaking the body", reach the same spot again. It helps to concentrate on a spot which one tries to keep an eye on for a considerable time and which one tries to look at again as soon as possible rather than to concentrate on the success of the *turn* itself. It is important to keep the body together, i.e. to concentrate all tension equally along the vertical axis of the body.

5.6.3 Cross Turn

The *cross turn* is a *turn* on both feet like the *turn* described above, and starts from tightly crossed forward or backward foot positions. It is then turned on the balls of the feet and ends in the crossed or parallel closed foot position. Like the *pivot turn*, it is one of the easy *turns*.

Grade 2

Sequence of exercises "Cross Turn"   Notes on procedure

Starting position: 1st position parallel, arms in neutral position.

PHASE 1
1. *Step* to the right side on straight leg, open arms for 2nd position *(préparation)* - place left foot crossed on balls of feet behind the right leg then *plié* and close left arm for 1st position.
Repeat for the other side.

Make sure in this *preparation* to put the weight over both feet in the crossed position, since the *cross turn* which follows is a *turn* on both feet, i.e a two-footed take off.

PHASE 2

2. For *préparation* see above - half *turn* on the balls of both feet to the left side, also closing the right arm for 1st position. After the *turn* the left foot crosses in front of the right foot. *Repeat continuously, then for the other side.*

3. For *préparation* see above - full *turn* on the balls of both feet to the left side, for position of arms and feet see above. *Repeat continuously or for the other side.*

Eyes always spot the new direction, pull feet together crossed.

Head control and tension as in other full *turns*.

PHASE 3

Combine both directions of *turns* smoothly one with the other.

5.6.4 Pas de Bourré and Turn en dehors

The *pas de bourré* is used here as *préparation*. The *turn en dehors* is a *turn* on one leg and requires a great amount of body tension, balance, head control, arm movement and much more time for practice than the *turns* described above. For other forms of exercises and exact technical details see the *catalogue of exercises of BERNARD*, pp. 80/81.

Grade 2 ↑

Sequence of exercises
"Turn en dehors"   Notes on procedure

Starting position: weight over the left leg, right leg in in sideward *tendu* position, arms in 2nd position.

The *spatial motive* of this step is: cross - side - open diagonally forwards and at the same time: up - up - down.
The *rhythmical motive* is : short - short - long, or: 1 and 2 in 2/4 rhythm.

PHASE 1

1. *Pas de bourré: step* to the right side on balls of feet cross behind left leg, close both arms for 1st position - small step to the left side on balls of feet - step to the right side diagonally across forwards into spatial direction 2 open with *plié*, left arm forwards and right arm sidewards.
Repeat for the other side.

2. *Pas de bourré* on the right side (*préparation*) - transfer weight onto the right leg and stretch, left leg *passé* parallel, close arms for 1st position - remain in balance.
Repeat for the other side.

3. See 2., now move into *relevé* on the right leg (respectively on the left leg) after the *préparation* and remain in balance.
Repeat for the other side.

In all the exercise take 4 cts. for one direction.

The degree of the turns becomes gradually larger. It is always important to practise spotting to help orientation in the new direction. *Préparation and turn* take 4 cts. each.

PHASE 2

4. See 3., now take off with quarter *turns* to the left respectively to the right side - place free leg next to supporting leg and repeat continuously.

5. Make the exercise more challenging through quarter *turns*, half *turns* and full *turns*.

PHASE 3

6. *Pas de bourré* to the right side - quarter *turn* to the left side.
- *Pas de bourré* to the left side - half *turn* to the right side.
- *Pas de bourré* to the right side - three quarter *turn* to the left side.
- *Pas de bourré* to the left side - one *turn* to the right side.
Repeat for the other side.

The degrees and the directions of the *turns* can be combined in many ways; advanced dancers can do two *turns*.

5.7 Isolation and Polycentrics

To round off the 5th section, a few examples are described of how to broaden the isolated combinations of movements *polycentrically* within one centre (see *Model Lessons 1+2*).

Here, with regard to the rhythmical-dynamic coordination of different centres, the imagination of teachers or trainers is not restricted in any way. They should be based on the music chosen, the current trend and the level of the group.

5.7.1 Head and Feet

Grade 2

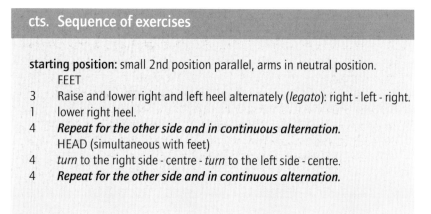

cts.	Sequence of exercises
	starting position: small 2nd position parallel, arms in neutral position.
	FEET
3	Raise and lower right and left heel alternately (*legato*): right - left - right.
1	lower right heel.
4	*Repeat for the other side and in continuous alternation.*
	HEAD (simultaneous with feet)
4	*turn* to the right side - centre - *turn* to the left side - centre.
4	*Repeat for the other side and in continuous alternation.*

Notes on procedure
- First feet and head can be practised separately, then simultaneously coordinated *polycentrically*. Head and feet move at the same rhythm but their dynamics are different. While the feet are rolled up and down in a smooth continuous movement (*legato*), the head is *turned* with accentuation (*staccato*).

5.7.2 Shoulders and Arms

Grade 2

cts.	Sequence of exercises

Starting position: 2nd position parallel, arms in neutral position.

2   raise and lower right shoulder with *push hand.*

2   raise and lower left shoulder with *push hand.*

4   raise right shoulder - raise left shoulder - lower right shoulder - lower left shoulder with *push hand.*

8   on cts. 1+2 circle right shoulder backwards - on cts. 3+4 circle right elbow backwards - on cts. 5+6 circle right arm backwards - on cts.7+8 pull elbow in towards the body centre and execute full *turn* to the left side on both feet (*contract*) - open legs for 2nd *jazz position* standing, spatial direction 8, right arm straight and inwardly rotated in 1st *jazz position*, left hand touches the groin.

4   bounce right shoulder backwards 2 times - on 2 cts. pull arm forwards in the process.

4   *repeat*

4   cts. 1-3 large arm circle backwards with *jazz hand* - on ct. 4 *turn* into 2nd *jazz position* standing in spatial direction 2.

4   cts. 1-3: 3 *shoulder shakes* right - left - right with *flat back* forwards, on ct. 4: straighten up for starting position in spatial direction 1. *Repeat whole sequence for the other side.*

Notes on procedure

- Execute the movement in *staccato*. When raising the shoulder, the arm remains hanging loosely; when lowering the shoulder, the bent hand *pushes* down.
- During the elbow circle the hand rests on the shoulder.
- Very rapid movement with an accentuated "Stop" in the final position.
- For 2nd *jazz position* see "*pliés*", 4th sequence of exercises.
- Alternate between *staccato* and *legato* execution.
- *Shoulder shakes* can be executed at double speed at advanced levels and thus be *multiplied*.

5.7.3 Chest and Arms

Grade 3

cts.	Sequence of exercises 1

Starting position: 2nd position parallel, arms in neutral position.

8   on cts. 1+2 *shift* chest to the right side.
On cts. 3+4 *shift* chest to the left then to the right side.
On cts. 5+6 *shift* chest to the left side.
On cts. 7+8 *shift* chest to the right side and develop right arm to the side.

4   tilt chest to the left side, right arm pulls - straighten up and do arm circle from the outside to the inside overhead (*"shampoo"*) - *turn* into spatial direction 8, legs in 2nd *jazz position*, chest *contracted*, bent forearms face forwards with fist.

4   on cts. 1+2 *release* chest, open arms to the sides, *flex* hands - on cts. 3+4 *contract* chest, close arms again (see above).

4   on cts. 1+2 *release* chest, open arms to the sides, *flex* hands - on ct. 3 *contract* chest, close arms again (see above) - on ct. 4 stretch legs and torso, raise arms for 3rd position, palms face forwards.

4   one deep *release* swing forwards and up.

4   one deep *release* swing forwards and up with frontal *turn* in spatial direction 1 and move arms to the sides and lower them.
Repeat whole sequence for the other side.

Notes on procedure
- Smooth continuous movement (*legato*). Body weight remains centred over both legs throughout, fix the pelvis.
- Execute the movement rapidly and with vigorous dynamics.
- Vigorously pulled movements. Weight over both legs.
- The torso *swing* is executed in the 2nd *jazz position* with a *release* at the respective *turning* point. Make sure to *release* the head well!

cts. Sequence of exercises 2

Starting position: 2nd position turned out, arms in neutral position.
CHEST
16 shift chest 15 times to the right side and to the left side, on
ct. 16 neutral position.
ARMS simultaneously.
4 cts. for *jazz port de bras* with right arm: bend the forearm in
front of the chest - place vertically - stretch arm up - lower straight
arm for 2nd position.
4 cts. for *jazz port de bras* with left arm: (see above)
8 cts.: 6 cts. for *jazz port de bras* with both arms **successively**,
starting with the right arm. Cts. 7+8: pause with the right arm,
left arm follows into same position - lower both arms.

Notes on procedure
- All movements are executed in accentuated *staccato*.
- This sequence can first be practised with both arms simultaneously since the
  successive execution is a very complicated form of coordination.

5.7.4 Pelvis, Steps, Arms and Head

Grade 2

cts. Sequence of exercises 1

Starting position: 2nd position parallel, arms in neutral position.
PELVIS
4 2 times *hip shift* to the right side - 2 times *hip shift* to the left side.
ARMS: right arm moves towards the side and up into V-position -
left arm moves towards the side and up into V-position
PELVIS
4 4 times *hip shift* right and left alternately. *ARMS:* right arm moves
into 2nd position with *push hand* - left arm moves into 2nd position
with *push hand* - right arm into neutral position - left arm into
neutral position.

4   PELVIS AND STEPS
Two side steps to the right side with *hip shift* to the left side (and *leg rotation*), with the last step do a quarter *turn* to the right. *ARMS:* left arm 2 times *push arm* to the side, right hand touches groin, after the *turn* close straight arm in front of chest. *HEAD:* *turn* 2 times to the left and to the centre.
4   PELVIS
On cts. 1+2: 2 times *contract-release*, counting style: "and 1 - and 2". *HEAD:* nod 2 times to the left side, cts. 3+4: *release* arms and *pas de bourré* with the left arm with half a *turn* to the left into neutral position.
Repeat whole sequence for the other side.

Notes on procedure
- The hip is bounced 2 times, whereas the arm is pulled in a continuous movement (*polyrhythmics*).
- Arm movement *staccato*.
- Fast and accentuated head and pelvis movements, *staccato*.

EPILOGUE

I would like to thank

Alain Bernard, who commissioned me to write the manuscript for Poland, for his collection of exercises, his corrections, his hospitality and for letting me use his library, Michael Korbl, without whose friendly help with the computer I would not have been able to write this book, my friend Susanne Wagner, who proofread the manuscript so many times and who gave me continuous encouragement to go on, the members of my dance group at Mainz University, who served as models, as a group and individually, for the photos, Wim Fischer, who took all the photos, and especially my son Martin, who developed hundreds of illustrations for me on the computer.

6 APPENDIX

Abbreviations

cts.   counts
Fig.   Figure

Technical Terms

arabesque   extending and raising the straight leg backwards
arabesque fall   arabesque and fall onto the stomach
attitude   one leg is bent to about 135 degrees

battement   extension of the leg that brushes the foot along the floor
bouncing *pliés*   bouncing the legs
breathings   coordination of breathing and movement
brushes, see *tendu* brush the straight leg out to the toe tip and lock leg
                    in again

centre work   working in standing positions
contraction fall fall with *contraction*
contraction plié *contraction*, legs bent, heels raised
contraction walk step with *contraction*
cou-de-pied   bringing the foot of the free leg next to the front of
                    the supporting leg

demi plié   bending the legs (small lowering of the centre of
                    gravity with upright torso), heels remain on the floor
développé   developing the free leg into straight position

flat back back bend   bending backwards with *flat back*
flatbacks   bending forwards or sideways with the back straight
                    and parallel to the floor
flex-point   bending-extending the feet
front fall   fall onto the stomach

grand plié   bending the legs to their maximal point (great
                    lowering of the centre of gravity with upright torso),
                    heels raised

high *release*	large back bend of the body
hop	jump on one leg
horizontal swings/ shifts	swinging the torso from one side to the other in table top position
jazz lunge	advancing one foot as far as possible with the knee bent and directly over the instep while the other foot remains stationary
jazz split	half-position on the floor, with the front leg straight and the rear leg bent
jazz walks	the jazz walk is a step which is longer than the natural stride
laterals	bending the torso to one side after shifting the hip
lay out	changing the position of the torso from the vertical position over one supporting leg and one raised leg
leg fortification	strengthening the leg muscles
leg swings and laterals	swinging the legs and bending the torso to one side
lunge position	see jazz lunge
pas de bourrée	cross - side - front ((cf. Jump into..., p.58))
passé	toe as high as the height of the knee ((cf. Jump into..., p.41, "Attidude"
pliés	bending and stretching the knees
port de bras	movements of the arms
préparation	preparatory phase of jumps, turns etc.
release swings	swinging the torso from one side to the other
relevé	rise into ball stand/ toe stand
side walk	step towards one side
slides	sliding on one or both legs
split fall	split and fall onto the stomach
step-tip	movement of the foot unweighted
turn en dedans	turn in the direction of the supporting leg (inside)
turn en dehors	turn in the direction of the free leg (outside)

LIST OF CDs

Annie Lennox: "Diva"	BMG, PD 75326
Brent Lewis: "Earth Tribe Rhythms"	KAUMA RECORDS
Eric Clapton: "Unplugged"	REPRISE 9362-45024-2
Laid Back: "Hole in Sky"	BMG 260263
Lionel Ritchie: "Back to the Front"	MOWTOWN 530018-2
Phil Collins: "But Seriously"	WEA 256984-2
Pili Pili: "Stolen Moments"	JARO 8648
Shakatak: "Turn the Music up"	POLYDOR 841077-2
Sidney Youngblood: "Feeling Free"	CIRCA, CIRD 9
Zaka Percussion: "Le Chant du Monde"	HARMONIA MUNDI; LDC 274.812

BIBLIOGRAPHY

ARBEITSGEMEINSCHAFT FÜR KLASSISCHEN TANZ AM UNGARISCHEN
STAATLICHEN BALLETT: Methodik des Klassischen Tanzes, Wilhelmshafen
1978
ACOGNY, GERMAINE: Danse Africaine, African Dance. Afrikanischer Tanz, Dakar
1918
CARLBLOM V., INGEBORG: Tänzerische Bewegungserziehung in der Krankengym-
nastik, Stuttgart, New York 1992
COHAN, ROBERT: The Dance Workshop, London 1986
FISCHER-MÜNSTERMANN, UTA: Von der Jazzgymnastik zum Jazztanz, Celle 1975
FRICH, ELISABETH: Matt Mattox – Jazz Dance, Weingarten 1984
FORSYTHE, A. M., PERCES, M. B., BELL, C.: The Dance Technique of Lester Horton,
Princeton 1992
GIARDANO, GUS: Anthology of American Jazz Dance, New York 1975
GIARDANO, GUS: Jazz Dance Class, Pennington 1992
GRIMMER, M.; GÜNTHER, H.: Theorie und Praxis des Jazz Dance, Stuttgart 1972
GÜNTHER, HELMUT: Jazzdance – Geschichte/Theorie/Praxis, Berlin 1980
GÜNTHER, HELMUT: Grundphänomene und Grundbegriffe des Afrikanischen und
Afroamerikanischen Tanzes, Graz 1969
HOROSKO, MARIAN: Martha Graham: The Evolution of her Dance Theorie and
Training 1926-1991, Pennington USA 1991
KNEBEL, KARL-PETER: Funktionsgymnastik, Reinbek bei Hamburg 1987
KUHN, WOLFGANG: Funktionelle Anatomie des menschlichen Bewegungsappa-
rates, Schorndorf 1979
MEINEL, KURT: Bewegungslehre, Berlin 1987
PETTERSON, KENDALL F., KENDALL MCCREARY, E.: Muskeln, Funktionen und
Tests, Stuttgart, New York 1988
SCHWABOWSKI, BRZANK, NICKLAS: Rhythmische Sportgymnastik, Aachen 1992
TITTEL, K.: Beschreibende und Funktionelle Anatomie des Menschen, Stuttgart,
New York 1990
TRAGUTH, FRED: Modern Jazz Dance, Bonn 1977
WAGANOWA, A. J.: Grundlagen des klassischen Tanzes, Velber bei Hannover
1966